So You Want to Move to CANADA, Eh?

So You Want to Move to CANADA, Eh?

STUFF TO KNOW BEFORE YOU GO

JENNIFER McCARTNEY

RUNNING PRESS
PHILADELPHIA

Running Press
Hachette Book Group
1290 Avenue of the Americas, New York, NY 10104
www.runningpress.com
@Running_Press

Printed in the U.S.A.

First Edition: June 2019

Published by Running Press, an imprint of Perseus Books, LLC, a subsidiary of Hachette Book Group, Inc. The Running Press name and logo is a trademark of the Hachette Book Group.

The Hachette Speakers Bureau provides a wide range of authors for speaking events. To find out more, go to www.hachettespeakersbureau.com or call (866) 376-6591.

The publisher is not responsible for websites (or their content) that are not owned by the publisher.

Print book cover and interior design by Susan Van Horn.
Map art on pages x and xi credit: Denys/Getty Images Plus
Plaid pattern: Getty Images Plus
Knit pattern credit: olgagriga/Getty Images Plus

Library of Congress Control Number: 2018964334

ISBNs: 978-0-7624-9507-8 (paperback), 978-0-7624-9506-1 (ebook)

LSC-C

10 9 8 7 6 5 4 3 2 1

FOR MY PARENTS,
TERRY AND REBECCA,
WHO CHOSE CANADA AS
THEIR HOME.

"Our population is shrinking. A slow economy, in combination with out-migration has us on an unsustainable path. . .

The truth is we welcome all, no matter the ideology. We have a beautiful island, a friendly people, a rich culture and a bright future."

—A tongue-in-cheek press release from the Canadian Island of Cape Breton after the 2016 US election, offering a safe haven to American "refugees"

CONTENTS

YUKON
NORTHWEST TERRITORIES
NUNAVUT
BRITISH COLUMBIA
ALBERTA
SASKATCHEWAN
MANITOBA

provinces and territories of CANADA

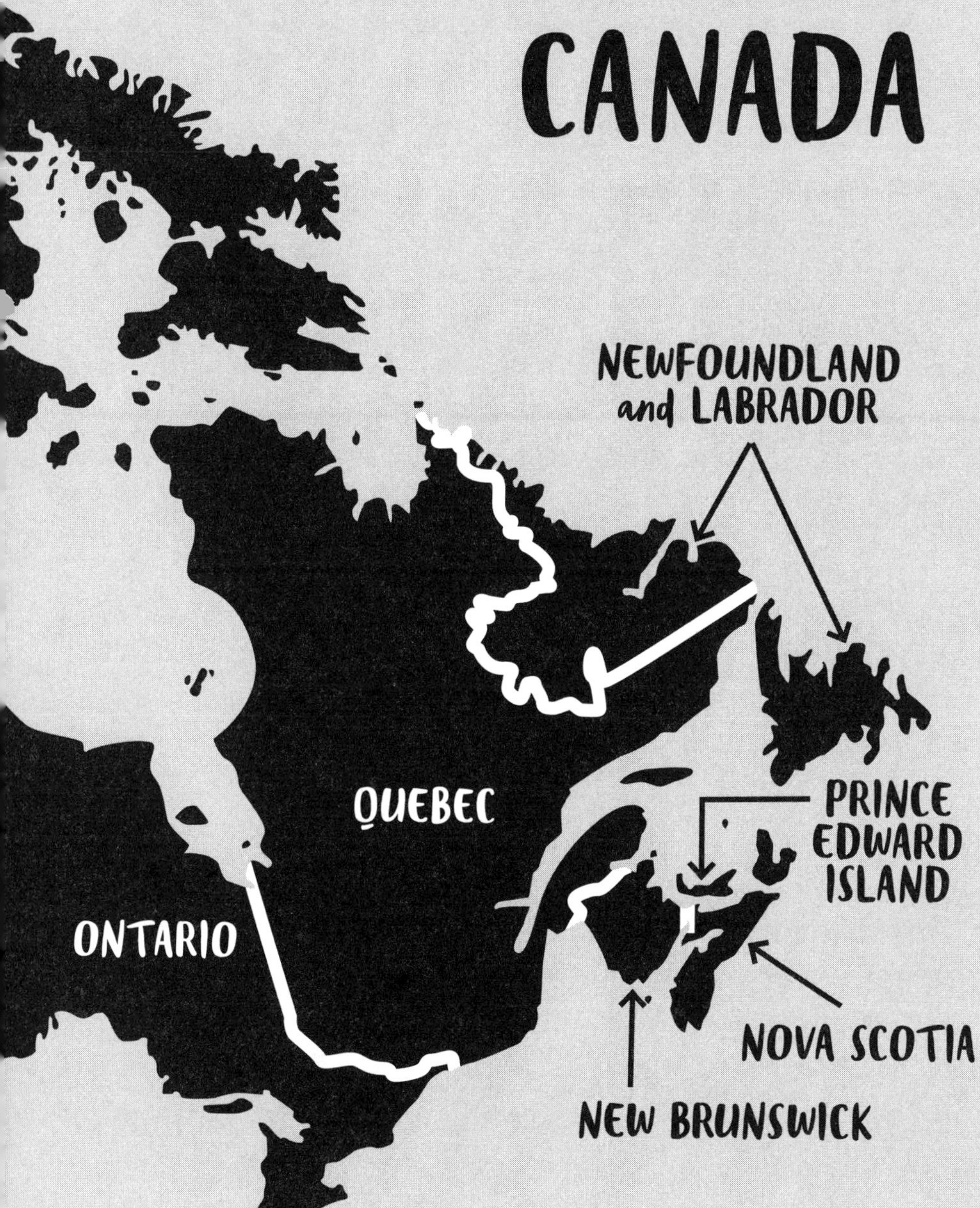

INTRODUCTION

WHAT'S YOUR CANADA FANTASY? Living life as an artist in an eco-cabin on Salt Spring Island? As a hotshot financier with a condo on the fifty-third floor of a posh building overlooking the Toronto skyline? As a quiet farmer in the rural Quebec countryside who supplies produce to all the hottest restaurants in Montreal? Or perhaps your fantasy involves a lumberjack. Or just free health care. Whatever your taste, it makes perfect sense to daydream about picking up and reinventing yourself in a country that's not only welcoming to newcomers but also affordable, safe, and, well, right next door.

Sometimes we're inspired to make a change after noteworthy events in our lives, such as a marriage or divorce, a death in the family, or a new job opportunity. Sometimes these noteworthy events that inspire us are more global in scale. Hours after the 2016 presidential election results were announced, for example, the Canadian immigration website crashed. Americans who supported the losing candidate wanted to know how to move to Canada—and fast. Even before that, searches for "How can I move to Canada" shot up 350 percent after the then-presidential nominee clinched the Republican nomination. And why not? It's nearby. It's a great place to live. The health care is famously free, the crime rate is low, and the quality of life—and the life expectancy—is high. In fact, three out of the top ten best cities to live in the world are in Canada, according to the 2017 Global Livability Report.

But how to go from a cursory internet search to concrete action? What's the first step? And what else do you really need to know in order to move there? The answer is: quite a bit if you want to immerse yourself in the full Canadian experience—which isn't just buying a flannel shirt and learning about the Canadian Football League,[1] although that's a great start.

"Geography has made us neighbors. History has made us friends. Economics has made us partners. And necessity has made us allies. Those whom nature hath so joined together, let no man put asunder."

John F. Kennedy,
address to the Canadian Parliament, 1961

There are a lot of stereotypes about Canada—many of them well earned. There's tons of space, and it's all kept pretty clean. The government is mostly honest and well meaning. The people are mostly laid back and well educated. It's a multicultural wonderland where everyone is welcome. Right? Aside from the health care and gun stuff, it's basically just like the United States in every other respect . . . isn't it? Well, not quite.

From our love of bunny hugs and chesterfields to our embrace of big government, strong rye, and . . . curling, there are a ton of

---

1   Argos suck.

subtle and not-so-subtle cultural differences newcomers to Canada will discover. Not to mention our uniquely Canadian history—moose on the loose in Tim Hortons, socialists on strike in Winnipeg, and crack-smoking mayors in Toronto. So you want to move to Canada? Buckle up! You've got a lot to learn. (And a lot of paperwork to fill out— we're a very bureaucratic country.)

Whether you're an armchair traveler, you've fallen in love with a Canadian, or you're simply fed up and ready for a real change, you'll enjoy this handy guide on what to expect. Written by a Canuck with dual American-Canadian citizenship, this is an authoritative and step-by-step practical guide on how to move to the best country in the world.[2]

---

2   First thing you'll learn: We're really not that modest. We think we're fantastic.

beaver

Montreal
bagel

snowmobile

x

d

ngues

Vietnamese
Pho
???

Keanu on skates

The
quee

The Sourtoe

poutir

Justin
Trudeau +
eber)

sss

Bear
spray

French stop sign

ARRÊT

maple
leaf

acorn

toqu

ouble

double

rye whisky

pine trees

CN Tower
(not to
scale)

garlic
dipping
sauce

eat
me

Pizza
Pizza

moose burger

hockey

loon

nne
ith
n "e"

Kiss the cod

kilometres

canoe

1$

loonie

???

Boxi
Da

CANADA AT A GLANCE

How Many Provinces Are There?
What's a Province?
And What's the Deal with the Queen?

"The more I see of the country, the less I feel I know about it. There is a saying that after five years in the north every man is an expert; after ten years, a novice."

—Pierre Berton, author

BASIC CANADIAN GEOGRAPHY

"Canada is like an old cow. The West feeds it. Ontario and Quebec milk it. And you can well imagine what it's doing in the Maritimes."

— Tommy Douglas

The country of Canada was founded more or less on July 1, 1867. Today Canada has ten provinces and three territories and is the world's second-largest country after Russia. There are vast differences among the provinces and territories, and each one has their own history as well as quirks and traditions. The story of how this gigantic landmass became the country of Canada is a bit disjointed—between Upper Canada and Lower Canada and the Hudson's Bay Company and a bunch of disparate colonies and unceded Indigenous land plus a few wars with the US Army, it wasn't exactly a straight path to nationhood. Read on to discover how each bit of Canada came to be (as well as recommendations for music, literature, and films that will offer additional insight into the culture of each province and territory—for more, see the additional resources starting on page 155).

CANADA: PURE POETRY

"Birth of Canada as a Nation, July First, 1867" is a poem by James McIntyre honoring the founding of Canada. McIntyre was unkindly known as Canada's "cheese poet" and mocked for his lack of literary talent. But this is a nice, historic little poem that manages to mention both beavers and maple trees, and it's also in the public domain, so here you are.

Hail Britannia's noblest daughter,
Who is surrounded by the water
Of many a lake and broad sea,
Land of beaver and of maple tree.
Her lofty brow is wreathed with smiles,
For from the far Atlantic isles
In pomp have come their delegates,
All seeking to unite their fates.
With Canada great northern queen,
And now throughout the land is seen,
High festival and stately dance,
Triumphant nuptials to advance.
And soon shall Red River valley
And distant Vancouver rally,
To form this Empire gigantic
From Pacific to Atlantic.

Beaver!

NEWFOUNDLAND AND LABRADOR

CAPITAL: St. John's

First, a lesson in pronunciation: "Newfoundland" rhymes with "understand." Learn that one thing, and you'll immediately endear yourself to the locals. Newfoundland and Labrador is one of the most interesting provinces geographically because it's closer to Ireland than it is to much of the rest of Canada, which means residents have slightly Irish-sounding accents, a cutting sense of humor, and incredible musical talent. Sea shanties, love ballads, fiddling, accordions, step dancing—you name it, and you'll find it here. Most likely in a pub. You'll also find whale, bird, and iceberg watching; picturesque villages overlooking the Atlantic; and moose burgers. It was the last province to join Canada, with 52 percent of residents voting to join in 1949. Those who voted against joining are still a bit salty about it all. They felt everything was fine as it was.

And it was here, in the town of Gander, that thirty-eight airplanes were forced to land after US airspace was shut down on September 11, 2001. There were more people on the planes than there were in town, but locals from all over the province banded together to cook food, donate supplies, fill prescriptions, feed the numerous animals in the cargo hold of each plane, and offer comfort for the thousands of passengers stranded there for days. Local stores told passengers to come in and take what they needed at no charge. Residents opened their homes to allow passengers to shower and use the phone. Lifelong friendships were formed during this difficult time. This astonishing story of generosity has since been immortalized in the award-winning Broadway musical *Come from Away*.

Be sure to head out to Cape Spear and catch the first sunrise in North America from the continent's most easterly point.

LISTEN: Great Big Sea

READ: *Death on the Ice: The Great Newfoundland Sealing Disaster of 1914* by Cassie Brown with Harold Horwood, or *The Colony of Unrequited Dreams* by Wayne Johnston

WATCH: *The Republic of Doyle*

PRINCE EDWARD ISLAND (also known as P.E.I.)

anne with an "e."

CAPITAL: Charlottetown

Canada's smallest province, both in terms of landmass and population, is a dreamy, picturesque island of about 140,000 people. It's a bit larger than the state of Delaware, if that means anything to you. The province is known for its delicious potatoes and oysters, fabulous beaches, and traditional Celtic music. This little island has an outsized spot in Canadian history, as the Charlottetown Conference was held here in 1864. This is where representatives from the various British colonies in North America got together to discuss forming one big union that would eventually become Canada. It was apparently a bit of a haphazard affair, with Newfoundland being notified too late to join the proceedings and a big circus in town hogging all the accommodations. The island is also known as the setting for one of Canada's most famous novels, *Anne of Green Gables* by Lucy Maud Montgomery. It's connected to the New Brunswick mainland by Confederation Bridge, the longest bridge in the world over a body of water that freezes.

LISTEN: Saddle River String Band

READ: *Anne of Green Gables* by Lucy Maud Montgomery

WATCH: *Road to Avonlea*

NOVA SCOTIA

CAPITAL: Halifax

Nova Scotia (Latin for New Scotland) was one of the four founding provinces of Canada and is located on a peninsula surrounded by the Atlantic. You're never more than sixty-seven kilometers (almost forty-two miles) from the ocean here, so it makes sense that the province is known for its fresh lobster and seafood. The area received a large number of Scottish settlers after the Highland clearances, which is why fiddle music is popular and Gaelic is still spoken in some communities. The Halifax explosion also occurred here—to date Canada's greatest disaster, with around two thousand killed and nine thousand injured when a munitions ship blew up in Halifax Harbor. It was, at the time, the world's largest man-made explosion—part of the unfortunate ship's anchor was found two miles south—and hospitals were quickly overwhelmed with the injured. Nova Scotia is also known for its two rather famous islands, Cape Breton and Sable Island. The former is the home of Louisbourg Fort, which played a pivotal role in the French and English wars, and it's also the site of Alexander Graham Bell and Marconi's groundbreaking experiments. The latter is a tiny sandspit managed by the federal government and known for its adorable wild horse population—about four hundred horses roam free on the foggy little island.

LISTEN: Stan Rogers or the Rankin Family

READ: *Barometer Rising* by Hugh McClelland, *No Great Mischief* by Alistair MacLeod, or *Heave* by Christy Ann Conlin

WATCH: *Maudie* or *Trailer Park Boys*

"Canadians, like their historians, have spent too much time remembering conflicts, crises, and failures. They forgot the great, quiet continuity of life in a vast and generous land. A cautious people learns from its past; a sensible people can face its future. Canadians, on the whole, are both."

—British military officer Desmond Morton

NEW BRUNSWICK

Capital: Fredericton

New Brunswick is one of the four Atlantic provinces and is the only officially bilingual—French and English—province in Canada, a great trivia fact because most people assume the official bilingual province must be Quebec. Inhabited since at least 7000 BC by Indigenous peoples like the Mi'kmaq, the first European contact was with French explorer Jacques Cartier, and the land eventually became part of the French colony of Acadia. When the British took over, they expelled the Acadians from the land in an act known as the Great Upheaval. In fact, the descendants of some of those displaced Acadians became today's modern-day Cajuns in Louisiana. The province is known for its beautiful forested landscapes (and its forestry industry) and the UNESCO-designated Bay of Fundy, which has the highest tides in the world. Come for the puffin and whale watching, stay for the delicious fiddleheads.

> **LISTEN:** Stompin' Tom Connors or Matt Anderson
>
> **READ:** *The Nine Lives of Charlotte Taylor* by Sally Armstrong
>
> **WATCH:** *Still Mine*

QUEBEC

Capital: Québec City

Quebec is our largest province and has a long, rich, and complicated history. It's also got some of the best food, art, and architecture in the country as a result of that history. If you're not from Canada, your knowledge of Quebec may be limited to the fact that people there speak French (and to piggy-back on the earlier trivia fact: it is the only province in Canada where French is the *sole* official language). That's a good start. But it's also important to know that for any prime minister to win a federal election, they're going to need to speak fluent French, participate in an all-French debate, and generally keep the left-leaning province happy. This reality isn't always popular with the rest of Canada, but that's the way it is. Why? Quebec was originally the French colony of New France, and it was the center of the lucrative fur trade from the early 1600s. It was populated largely by Roman Catholic settlers, European explorers, and the requisite priests and nuns. Then in 1759, during the Seven Years' War, just outside the walls of Québec City, the French and English armies fought the Battle of the Plains of Abraham. The British won, and the French eventually ceded all their land to the Brits. To ensure they didn't have an uprising of pissed-off French people, the British strategically protected the existing French system of civil law, its Roman Catholic religion, and its language and customs, letting everyone get on pretty much the same as they always had. The effects of this policy can still be felt today. The province's official language is French, for example, and road signs are in French only.

Lots more has happened in Quebec over the years, including an American invasion in 1775 (the United States lost); the October Crisis in 1970, when French militants kidnapped and murdered the deputy premier of Quebec, Pierre Laporte; and the 1995 referendum on sovereignty when Quebecers narrowly voted to remain part of Canada. Today the province has a large Anglophone population as well as many new Canadians with a first language other than French or English. It's a unique tourist destination where visitors can catch a jazz festival in Montreal, take in some seventeenth-century art in Québec City, and generally eat and drink their way through the beautiful countryside (rabbit poutine anyone?).

Listen: Leonard Cohen

Read: *The Apprenticeship of Duddy Kravitz* by Mordecai Richler or *Cockroach* by Rawi Hage

Watch: *Jesus of Montreal* or *Bon Cop Bad Cop*

ONTARIO

Capital: Toronto

Ontario is the country's most populous province, with about thirteen million residents—which means about 38 percent of all Canadians live here. It's also home to Toronto, the country's biggest city and the national capital of Ottawa. Below it are the states of Minnesota, Michigan, Ohio, Pennsylvania, and New York; to the east is Quebec; and to the west, Manitoba. It's named after Lake Ontario, thought to be either a Huron word meaning "great lake" or an Iroquois word meaning "beautiful water." The area was mostly settled by English-speaking Europeans and was known as Upper Canada for a while. After a couple of wars with the Americans, a bunch of government officials got together and decided they'd better make a proper country out of the land they currently controlled before the United States got any more ideas. Ontario became one of Canada's original provinces in 1867 along with Quebec, New Brunswick, and Nova Scotia.

With a quarter of a million freshwater lakes and loads of provincial parks, the more sparsely populated northern part of the province is huge—and a favorite destination for fishing, boating, hiking, and general relaxing. The southern part of the province, where most Ontarians reside (94 percent of them), is where you'll find Niagara Falls; big cities like Toronto, Brampton, Mississauga, Ottawa, Hamilton, London, and Kingston; and the busy US border crossings into Buffalo, New York and Detroit, Michigan. Industry includes pretty much everything: mining and forestry, arts and education, tourism, and banking and finance. There's also a large tech sector based in the city of Waterloo that's been dubbed Silicon Valley North because people like to name things.

Ontario is where you'll find the massive Six Nations reserve, which is home to six Iroquois nations (Cayuga, Mohawk, Oneida, Onondaga, Seneca, and the Tuscarora). The government's Haldimand Proclamation in 1784 "granted" them the land as a reward for fighting with the British during the American Revolution. Not surprisingly, the land promised in the original treaty has shrunk over the years as various new surveys were completed; nevertheless, it remains the largest reserve in Canada.

LISTEN: The Tragically Hip or A Tribe Called Red

READ: *In the Skin of a Lion* by Michael Ondaatje or *Alias Grace* by Margaret Atwood

WATCH: *Slings & Arrows* or *Kim's Convenience*

margaret atwood

TORONTO THE GOOD. T.O. T-DOT. THE SIX. HOGTOWN. QUEEN CITY.

As Canada's largest city, Toronto deserves a special mention—as much as this may annoy people who live elsewhere in Canada and feel like Toronto takes up all the oxygen. Since the area was first settled in 1750, it's become not only the country's most populous spot but also its cultural and financial hub too. More than 50 percent of Toronto's population was born outside of Canada, and there are more than 150 languages spoken here, making it one of the most multicultural cities in the world. It's got loads of museums and art galleries, six opera companies, numerous theaters, lots of universities, a bunch of newspapers and media outlets, two international airports, and, of course, restaurants for every taste. Toronto also has North America's oldest continuously operating theater, the Royal Alexandra Theatre, which opened in 1907. It's home to four major league sports teams—the Blue Jays, Raptors, Toronto Football Club, and Maple Leafs, as well as the Canadian Football League's Toronto Argonauts. Five national banks and the Toronto Stock Exchange are also headquartered here. It's kind of a big deal. Unless you don't live there, in which case you consider it totally overrated.

MANITOBA

CAPITAL: Winnipeg

Manitoba is smack in the middle of Canada and one of the three prairie provinces. It sits above Minnesota and North Dakota and extends all the way north to the territory of Nunavut.

Its original inhabitants included the Ojibwe, Dene, and Cree peoples. In its infancy the area was controlled by the Hudson's Bay Company and was called Rupert's Land. After confederation in 1867, the private company then ceded the land to Britain—to the dismay of many French settlers in the region.

This led to one of the most infamous incidents in Canadian history—the Métis uprising against the Canadian government in 1869. Louis Riel, who felt the new government was ignoring the concerns of his people, led the Red River Rebellion. Riel created a provisional Métis government and arrested—and executed—those considered pro-Canada. The resistance led to negotiations with the Canadian government, resulting in the founding of the modern province of Manitoba as well as religious and education protections for French speakers in the region. After a brief self-imposed exile in the United States, Riel came back to lead another rebellion in 1885. This time the Canadian government arrested and executed Riel for treason. The government eventually got over being pissed off about all this, and February 18 is now observed as Louis Riel Day in Manitoba.

The 1919 Winnipeg General Strike is another famous bit of history. Unemployment and inflation along with poor wages and dismal working conditions led the Winnipeg Trades and Labor Council (WTLC) to call a general strike. More than thirty thousand people walked off the job, closing factories and shops and disrupting train service. In solidarity, public-sector workers like the police, firemen, and postal workers also joined the strike. The federal government then stepped in to support the business owners and arrested labor organizers. After a skirmish with the police in which a striker was killed and thirty more injured, the unions voted to return to work, but the strike would inspire labor movements for years to come.

Winnipeg is the cultural hub of the province[3] and is also home to the Museum of Human Rights and Freedoms, where you can spend hours taking in all the exhibits—plus the building itself is great too. There's an established arts scene here as well. The Royal Winnipeg Ballet, for example, is the longest continually operating ballet company in North America. Polar bear enthusiasts are in luck as well, as the province is also the home of Churchill, the polar bear capital of the world.

Listen: Neil Young or the Weakerthans

Read: *The Stone Angel* by Margaret Laurence or *A Complicated Kindness* by Miriam Toews

Watch: *The Saddest Music in the World*

---

3 *Home Alone* was filmed here!**

**Okay, fine, it was *Home Alone: The Holiday Heist*. Otherwise known as *Home Alone 5*.

SASKATCHEWAN

Capital: Regina

Saskatchewan (*kisiskāciwani-sīpiy*) means "swift-flowing river" in Cree. The name is apt, as around 10 percent of the province is fresh water. It's also the location of Moose Jaw, which has to be one of the coolest place names in the country (apart from Medicine Hat and Dildo). This landlocked province is known for its agriculture and mining industry—mostly wheat as well as rye and lentils. It is also the world's largest exporter of mustard seed and . . . uranium. The Quebec aerospace company Bombardier has a large presence here as well. Like the American Midwest and West, much of the province was settled by Ukrainian, Polish, Scandinavian, and German immigrants,[4] whose influence is still felt today.

Historically Saskatchewan has been one of the nation's most progressive, thanks to its election of North America's first democratic socialist government in 1944—the Co-operative Commonwealth Federation (CCF). As a result, the province was the first to implement free Medicare for all in 1947 because of the efforts of

---

4   The Hantelman Building on the University of Saskatchewan campus is named after a relative of the author: farmer-turned-CCF member of Parliament, World War I veteran, and Iowa native Louis R. Hantelman. While awarding him an honorary law degree in 1955, the dean of agriculture said of Hantelman: "He has assisted many worthy students financially, usually as an anonymous donor. Mr. Hantelman is a pioneer who was here before Saskatchewan existed as a province; he is a leader in the field of farming and the progress and stability of agriculture; although not a native of Canada, he fought for her; he has had a distinguished record of service in public life; he has helped many and few knew where the help came from; he is a man of wisdom and generous heart."

Premier Tommy Douglas, a prairie preacher-turned-politician who later became the first leader of the federal New Democratic Party. (Alberta followed suit in 1950, and the rest of Canada got free universal health care by 1966.)

Fun fact: the hottest temperature ever recorded in Canada happened here in 1937, with a high of 45 degrees Celsius, or 113 degrees Fahrenheit.

Listen: Buffy St. Marie or the Sheepdogs

Read: *Who Has Seen the Wind* by W. O. Mitchell

Watch: *Little Mosque on the Prairie*

ALBERTA

Capital: Edmonton

Alberta is often described as the "Texas of Canada" due to its robust cattle farming and oil industries—the Athabasca oil sands produce over one million barrels of oil per day. As a result, the province is an economic powerhouse, with a per capita GDP in 2013 that exceeded that of the United States, Switzerland, or Norway. It's also home to dramatic Rocky Mountain scenery, with towns like Banff, Canmore, and Jasper bringing tourists from around the world to take in the turquoise lakes, glaciers, and mountain vistas. (If you follow any travel influencers on social media, you've probably seen a picture of them in a flowy dress or with a rumpled plaid shirt doing a yoga pose at Lake Louise.) It's also home to the world-renowned Banff Centre for the Arts, which hosts international artists for a variety of programs throughout the year.[5] The Alberta Badlands and Dinosaur Provincial Park are also tourist draws. While wildlife in Alberta no longer includes dinosaurs, they do have grizzly and black bears, mountain lions, lynx, and cougars.

Originally home to the Plains Cree, Blackfoot, and Chipewyan peoples, parts of the province after European contact became French, Spanish, English, and even American. The Hudson's Bay Company (a fur trading company) also claimed some of it. It became a Canadian province in 1905 and is named after Queen Victoria's sixth child, Princess Louise Caroline Alberta. After nearly fifty years with a progressive conservative government, residents elected the left-leaning New Democrats in 2015. Calgary's current mayor, Naheed Nenshi, elected in 2010, is the first Muslim mayor of any major North American city. He's worth following on Twitter if you get the chance: @nenshi.

LISTEN: k.d. lang or Jann Arden

READ: *The Black Grizzly of Whisky Creek* by Sid Marty

WATCH: *FUBAR*

---

5   It's great there. Every artist should apply now—you won't regret it.

BRITISH COLUMBIA
(also known as B.C.)

CAPITAL: Victoria

"Sat staring, staring, staring—half lost, learning a new language or rather the same language in a different dialect. So still were the big woods where I sat, sound might not yet have been born."

—Emily Carr, artist

British Columbia is Canada's westernmost province that sits above Washington, Idaho, and Montana and extends north to Alaska and the Yukon and Northwest Territories. Originally home to around two hundred nations, including the Haida and Tlingit (before most of them died in a smallpox epidemic), some of the world's most beautiful and important Indigenous art comes from here, such as totem poles, dugout canoes, and ceremonial masks. Like much of Canada, B.C. was settled by a mix of the Spanish, British, and French. Fort Victoria was established on Vancouver Island in 1843, and the British settlement eventually became the quaint capital city of Victoria, where you can still get high tea or a pint of bitter, depending on your taste. B.C. became a province in 1871. Most of B.C. is unceded territory, which means that, unlike much of eastern Canada, there were no land treaties between Indigenous peoples and the government, although this is slowly changing as new agreements are signed.

The province is also home to another and more recent shameful chapter in Canadian history. During World War II more than twenty-two thousand Canadian Japanese citizens living in B.C. were sent to internment camps far from the coast. Their forced relocation was funded by the sale of their own seized land and possessions. The federal government formally apologized in 1988. More recently the province is at the center of a dispute with the Canadian government, which wants to build an oil pipeline from neighboring Alberta to the coast of B.C.—an environmentally fragile area that critics reasonably argue would be devastated by tanker traffic and potential oil spills. There are ongoing protests and debates about the merits of the project, and it will likely be years before the issue is resolved.

British Columbia is also a province known for its natural beauty as well as the buzzing metropolitan city of Vancouver. In Vancouver (also known as Hollywood of the North due to its thriving film industry) you'll find healthy yoga-pant and fleece-wearing young professionals working hard to try to afford a one-bedroom condo in the city's astonishingly unaffordable housing market. Nearby in Whistler there's world-class skiing and snowboarding, while the inland Okanagan region offers award-winning wineries. With around six thousand islands and seventeen thousand miles of coastline, the province is perfect for boating, whale watching, fishing, and birding. Overall B.C. has a casual, eco-friendly, and free-wheeling vibe that's comparable, you might say, to California.

LISTEN: Sarah McLachlan or the Matthew Good Band

READ: *Obasan* by Joy Kogawa, *Golden Spruce* by John Valliant, or *Eating Dirt* by Charlotte Gill

WATCH: *The Beachcombers* or *The Sweet Hereafter*

YUKON

CAPITAL: Whitehorse

Yukon is the smallest of Canada's three territories and borders Alaska to the west, the Northwest Territories to the east, and British Columbia to the south. The region is largely defined by the Yukon River—the territory's namesake—with the capital city of Whitehorse located on its banks. It's home to Mount Logan, Canada's highest peak and the second highest in North America after Denali. English is primarily spoken here, perhaps due to the massive influx of more than one hundred thousand American prospectors who came here to seek their fortunes during the Klondike gold rush. Although hardly anyone struck it rich, the legacy of the gold rush lives on with Klondike Gold Rush National Historical Park; books by Jack London, Jules Verne, and Pierre Berton; and the film *Gold Rush* starring Charlie Chaplin. There's even an official holiday here called Discovery Day to honor the moment gold was found. Mining is still a large part of the economy today, although tourism is big too: you can see the northern lights from here, along with grizzly bears, caribou, lynx, elk, and arctic foxes. Or maybe try your hand at running the Yukon Arctic Ultra Marathon—a grueling 430-mile wilderness route with temperatures that can hit below -40 degrees Celsius (which is also -40 degrees Fahrenheit).

LISTEN: Kim Beggs

READ: *The Shooting of Dan McGrew* by Robert Service or any reporting on the region by journalist Eva Holland

WATCH: *Dawson City: Frozen in Time*

"This is the law of the Yukon, that only the Strong shall survive;

That surely the Weak shall perish, and only the Fit survive.

Dissolute, damned and despairful, crippled and palsied and slain,

This is the Will of the Yukon,—Lo, how she makes it plain!"

—Robert Service, *Law of the Yukon*

NORTHWEST TERRITORIES

CAPITAL: Yellowknife

This territory became part of Canada on July 15, 1870, but its modern-day borders were established in 1999 after its eastern lands became the new territory of Nunavut. Like its new next-door neighbor, the territory has a high percentage of Indigenous people who speak languages including Dogrib, North Slavey, and Dene. The lakes are notable: Great Slave Lake is the continent's deepest, and Great Bear Lake is Canada's largest. There are no political parties here—everyone is elected as an independent—and the territory uses a consensus system of government. Sounds civilized, doesn't it? The Northwest Territories is also the birthplace of the North-West Mounted Police, which became our modern-day Royal Canadian Mounted Police (RCMP). Prime Minister Sir John A. Macdonald established this early federal police force in 1873, and their first responsibilities included tamping down the Red River Rebellion and keeping the peace during the Klondike gold rush. They were also tasked with forcibly relocating Indigenous communities out of the way of the new national railway line.

The area's mining industry currently consists of gold, diamonds, and natural gas. The Yellowknife Airport is the main hub for other communities in the region. The Northwest Territories is also known for its popular music festivals, including the Great Northern Arts Festival and Folk on the Rocks.

LISTEN: Grey Gritt

READ: *Late Nights on Air* by Elizabeth Hay

WATCH: *North of 60*

NUNAVUT

CAPITAL: Iqaluit

The largest and newest territory in Canada, Nunavut was created in 1999 as a result of the Nunavut Land Claims Agreement Act. The territory, about the size of Mexico, is home to just over thirty-five thousand people. (With just one elected member of Parliament in the House of Commons, it's the world's largest electoral district.) Its inhabitants are primarily Inuit, a people who have continuously inhabited the land for more than four thousand years. Inuktitut is the most commonly spoken language here, and it's one of the territory's three official languages alongside English and French. It's also home to the world's most northern, permanently inhabited settlement, called Alert, as well as Baffin Island, Canada's largest. There is evidence of early Inuit contact with the Vikings before 1000 CE; however, due to its harsh climate, the area was left largely alone by later European settlers (at least compared to regions down south). The industries here are a mix of mining (iron ore and gold), hunting and fishing, whaling, tourism, and military stuff. During the Cold War the federal government was so worried about the vulnerability of its strategically important northern lands that it forcibly relocated Inuit from northern Quebec to populate the region. The government formally apologized for this in 2010.

The territory is known for its arctic climate, Indigenous culture, and arts scene, which includes the West Baffin Co-operative and the world-famous Kinngait Co-operative (formerly Cape Dorset Co-operative).

FUN FACT: Residents of Nunavut are called Nunavummiut.

LISTEN: Tanya Tagaq or the Jerry Cans

READ: *Sweetest Kulu* by Celina Kalluk and Alexandria Neonakis or *Those Who Run in the Sky* by Aviaq Johnston and Toma Feizo Gas

Watch: *Angry Inuk* or ᐊᑕᓇᕐᔪᐊᑦ *(Atanarjuat: The Fast Runner)*.

seal fur
mittens

BASIC NEED-TO-KNOW MEASUREMENTS

- -

Like most sane countries in the world, Canada uses the *metric system*. That means kilometres, metres, and centimetres. So when you see a sign with a speed limit of "100," that means kilometres, not miles, you maniac. And your twelve-ounce can of soda is now 325 millilitres of soda. Magic!

Get ready to hear the temperature in Celsius instead of Fahrenheit. There are clever ways to convert from one to the other in your head if you're some kind of math genius. You can look up those tricks if you're curious. But generally, it helps to remember that 20 degrees Celsius is about 70 degrees Fahrenheit—warm enough to wear shorts.

Canada uses the Canadian dollar. Its value fluctuates but is generally worth a bit less than the American dollar. There are no dollar bills in Canada, so get used to having forty pounds of change in your pockets. The dollar coin is called a loonie, and the two-dollar coin is called a toonie (more jargon like this on page 124). We don't have pennies anymore because they're pointless.

kilometres   litres

THE CANADIAN FLAG

If you've ever gone backpacking in Europe, you're likely familiar with the Canadian flag. Canadian travelers notoriously like to sew it onto their bags to help distinguish themselves from their US neighbors. (Just like you should never confuse a Scot for a Brit or a New Zealander for an Australian, God help the person who asks a Canadian, "What part of America are you from?") During the Bush years, some left-leaning American travelers also took up the practice and became honorary Canucks, mostly to avoid having to explain to Europeans that Americans weren't, in fact, all idiots.

maple leaf

Anyway, Canada's distinctive red-and-white maple-leaf flag was first unveiled in 1965. It replaced the more colonial-feeling Canadian Red Ensign, which featured the Union Jack and the Canadian coat of arms on a red background. Replacing the Red Ensign was controversial, however: the history books apparently refer to this as the Great Canadian Flag Debate—and a national paper even called it the Great Flag Farce. Generally, Conservatives and veterans wanted to keep the existing flag, while Prime Minister Pearson and the Liberals thought Canada should have a new design. One of the reasons for wanting a change was that the existing design wasn't popular in Quebec, and some foreign governments who liked Canada but not the UK didn't care for the fact that the Red Ensign featured the Union Jack.

So although it's hard to imagine today, picking a new flag was an
extremely divisive and tumultu-
ous process. The *Winnipeg Tribune*
noted in an editorial, "It would be
difficult to imagine anything more
divisive at the moment in Canada's
history than [Pearson's] apparent
obsession to introduce a new flag."
One irate citizen wrote to the prime
minister, "I think you are a traitor to the Commonwealth and should
be hauled up for treason. . . . Why on earth were you given the Nobel
Peace Prize, I'll never know."[6]

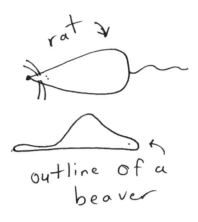

Amidst this controversy thousands of new flag design sugges-
tions poured in from the public. After many meetings, committees,
hearings, and debates, seven MPs from various parties voted on two
designs. Originally, of the 3,541 entries, 2,136 included maple leaves,
408 included Union Jacks, 389 had a beaver, and 359 had a fleur-de-
lis. Group of Seven artist A. Y. Jackson, who had submitted his own
design, explains the difficulties posed by the challenge: "We had to
decide on an emblem or an abstract design such as a tri-colour, and

---

6   Prime Minister Pearson was indeed awarded a Nobel Prize in 1957 for his role in
mediating the Suez Crisis, likely helping to prevent a major war. Pearson noted in
1955, "The fact is, that to every challenge given by the threat of death and destruction,
there has always been the response from free men: It shall not be. By these responses
man has not only saved himself, but has ensured his future. May it be so again this
time, as we face the awful and the glorious possibilities of the nuclear age."

there's so many of those it's hard to get a distinctive flag. We have no animal—the beaver looks like a rat—and so the maple leaf seems best."

The current maple leaf design by George Stanley was the unanimous winner. Another Group of Seven member, A. J. Casson, noted it "looks like some 6-year-old's effort in kindergarten." Pearson was pretty happy, though, saying, "Under this flag may our youth find new inspiration for loyalty to Canada; for a patriotism based not on any mean or narrow nationalism, but on the deep and equal pride that all Canadians will feel for every part of this good land."

Today Canadians love the design, and you'll see it on everything from throw pillows and T-shirts to mugs and shot glasses. And backpacks, of course. Unlike the United States, Canada doesn't have any laws governing how to treat the flag. We love and respect it, but it isn't quite deified the way the US flag is in some circles. Don't get me wrong—we can be as wildly patriotic as our southern neighbors, and come Canada Day, you'll see stores crammed with maple-leaf-themed merch. But on a regular afternoon in January, you likely won't find someone shopping for milk in a head-to-toe-patterned Canadian flag jumpsuit.

February 15 is designated Flag Day in Canada.

THE CANADIAN NATIONAL ANTHEM

Canada didn't get an official national anthem until 1980. Despite its rather late adoption by the Canadian government, "O Canada" is more than a hundred years old and was long considered an unofficial anthem of sorts—along with "God Save the Queen" and "The Maple Leaf Forever." First written in French in 1880 and with lyrics by Sir Adolphe-Basile Routhier and music by Calixa Lavallée, it wasn't translated into English until 1906. Robert Stanley Weir's English translation is now the official English version. But don't worry about remembering who wrote it: unlike America's Francis Scott Key, who's been given the hero's treatment in the history books, Canadians would be hard-pressed to tell you who wrote our anthem—I'd wager less than 10 percent of Canadians know this information.

You'll hear the anthem mostly at sporting events or government ceremonies. In fact, the American NHL team, the Buffalo Sabres, plays both the Canadian and American national anthems before every single game, regardless of whether they're playing a Canadian team. Located in a border town, the team wants to ensure it pays respects to its massive Canuck fan base.

In 2018 the English version of the anthem was slightly revised to become gender neutral. "In all thy sons command" became "in all of us command." This is actually in keeping with the original English lyrics that read "thou dost in us command," which were in turn revised in 1913 to add "thy sons." What can we say? Language is fluid, and we adapt with the times.

Here are the English lyrics:

O Canada!

Our home and native land!

True patriot love in all of us command.

With glowing hearts we see thee rise,

The True North strong and free!

From far and wide,

O Canada, we stand on guard for thee.

God keep our land glorious and free!

O Canada, we stand on guard for thee.

O Canada, we stand on guard for thee.

true patriot love

BASIC NEED-TO-KNOW GOVERNMENT

"Canada is the only country in the world where you can buy a book on federal-provincial relations at an airport."

—Michael Valpy, Canadian journalist

The queen

Canada is a federal constitutional monarchy, which means Queen Elizabeth II is still kind of our boss, although she's mostly a figurehead at this point. She's on the back of all our money, and you'll spot official portraits of her in our government institutions. The official royal representative in Canada is called the governor general.

Practically, though, the government runs independently of the Crown and operates as a parliamentary democracy like the UK. That means we've got multiple political parties. Citizens vote in federal elections for their local member of parliament (MP). If enough members from one party win at least 170 out of the 338 that are up for grabs, that party can form a government. If no one party gets a majority, it means a minority government, which is a complicated sort of thing that the average person probably couldn't fully explain.

Canadian citizens can register to vote online or through the mail.

CANADA'S FEDERAL POLITICAL PARTIES

Canada currently has four main federal parties. Only two of them have ever formed federal governments—the Liberals and the Conservatives. Because of the way the government is structured, however, the parties often must work together to accomplish their goals—two minority parties can band together to outvote the party in power, for example. For this reason politics in Canada tends to be less divisive than it is in the United States, where two main parties compete for power. In Canada there's a little more cooperation required in order to get stuff done.

THE CONSERVATIVE PARTY OF CANADA

*"Our Canada is an inclusive country, built by English-
and French-speaking Canadians, together with our
Aboriginal peoples, who were here first, and the millions who have come since from every corner of the
world. And still they come—one million people a year
make inquiries about coming to Canada."*

—Prime Minister Kim Campbell,
member of the Progressive Conservative Party

The Conservatives are a right-of-center political party formed in 2003. (Although historically there used to be several federal right-leaning parties, including the Alliance and Progressive Conservatives, it's now just one big party.) The party favors things like a more decentralized federal government, lower taxes, and expanded trade. Former Conservative prime ministers include Brian Mulroney and Stephen Harper. One of the party's legacies includes NAFTA, the North American Free Trade Agreement, signed by the Conservatives in 1994 and recently renegotiated in 2018.

THE LIBERAL PARTY OF CANADA

"There are few nations whose citizens cannot look to Canada and see their own reflection. For generations, men and women and families from the four corners of the globe have made the decision to choose Canada to be their home. Many have come here seeking freedom—of thought, religion and belief. Seeking the freedom simply to be."

—Prime Minister Paul Martin, member of the Liberal Party

The Liberals are a middle-of-the-road party—on most issues they are to the right of the New Democratic Party of Canada (NDP, see below) and to the left of Conservatives. Because of this centrism, the Liberal party is often seen as the most accommodating party, and indeed since 1918 the Liberals have won nineteen out of twenty-nine federal elections. Liberal prime ministers include Justin Trudeau and his father, Pierre Trudeau, as well as Jean Chrétien. Liberal legacies include the legalization of same-sex marriage and marijuana as well as the decision not to join the American-led invasion of Iraq.[7]

---

7   Yes, this is considered middle-of-the-road liberalism in Canada. Although many would argue these ideas originated with the country's leftist party, the NDP.

THE NEW DEMOCRATIC PARTY OF CANADA (NDP)

"Canada is a great country, one of the hopes of the world. We can be a better one—a country of greater equality, justice, and opportunity. We can build a prosperous economy and a society that shares its benefits more fairly. We can look after our seniors. We can offer better futures for our children. . . . Don't let them tell you it can't be done."

—NDP leader Jack Layton

The NDP is a left-of-center party that began as the CCF, a democratic socialist party founded by farmers and labor groups in 1932 in Calgary, Alberta. The party advocates for things like more robust spending on health care, early childhood education, and care for seniors as well as environmental protections and higher taxes on corporations. Although the NDP has formed numerous provincial governments, it has yet to form a federal one. Nonetheless, all Canadians today feel the impact of its provincial policies—the CCF introduced Canada's first universal health care plan in Saskatchewan in 1947, which eventually led to universal health care for all Canadians.

BLOC QUÉBÉCOIS

"Look at what has occurred in history. When the Berlin Wall fell, it was not surprising, but it was unexpected. Who predicted the Arab Spring? Nobody expected it, but all the ingredients were there. I think all the ingredients are also there for Quebec to become a country. But when? That's another question."

—Bloc Québécois leader Gilles Duceppe

The Bloc, as they're commonly called, is a Quebec-based party founded in 1991 that advocates solely for the interests of the province. It's a left-leaning, social democrat organization and also a separatist one—the party campaigned for the secession of Quebec during the 1995 referendum, and their platform today includes the promise to create an independent state. Aside from its separatist goals, the party pledges increased support for child care, the arts, and postsecondary education. The party's focus on independence has become controversial of late, and there are indications the party has fallen out of fashion a bit. In 2018 some elected members of the Bloc jumped ship and announced a new party called Quebec Debout, which would focus less on the issue of independence and more on promoting Quebec's interests within Canada; however, the new party dissolved a few months later.

GREEN PARTY

"I hold a vision of this blue green planet, safe and in balance. At the end of the Fossil Fuel Era, we are emerging to a new reality. We are ready to make the next leap—as momentous as abolishing slavery or giving women the vote,"

—Party leader Elizabeth May, member of the Green Party

Founded in 1983, the Green Party advocates for things like increased environmental protections, decreased military spending, mandatory labels for all genetically modified foods, and investment in renewable energy. Until recently the Green Party was largely viewed as a fringe party, in part because it had never elected a member to the House of Commons. However, with the election of candidate Elizabeth May in 2011, who was also the Green Party leader, the party rose in prominence. In the 2015 federal election, the party garnered 3.45 percent of the vote.

wind
turbine

A POLITICAL DISAGREEMENT ABOUT LIBRARIES

"Well, good luck to Margaret Atwood. I don't even know her. If she walked by me, I wouldn't have a clue who she is. She's not down here, she's not dealing with the problem. Tell her to go run in the next election and get democratically elected. And we'd be more than happy to sit down and listen to Margaret Atwood."

—Toronto city councilor **Doug Ford** in 2011, in response to Atwood's support for a campaign to keep Toronto libraries from losing funding

"I am not running for mayor yet. But if it comes to be true that people cannot voice an opinion unless they have been elected, then we are no longer in a democracy."

—Author Margaret Atwood's response, in the *Globe and Mail*, August 2, 2011

CANADIAN HOLIDAYS

Canada has its own unique holidays. Boxing Day is one of the best. The day after Christmas is our version of Black Friday, when everyone goes nuts at the sales. Also, Canadian Thanksgiving is earlier than yours. And Thanksgiving is not a huge deal here, so be prepared for no one to give a sh*t about the fact you can't find a forty-pound turkey at the grocery store—just serve ham and be done with it. We also don't have Columbus Day, Martin Luther King Day, or Memorial Day.

FAMILY DAY

Third Monday in February

This isn't a federal holiday, but it's celebrated as a provincial holiday in eight out of ten provinces. (In Manitoba it's called Louis Riel Day, in Nova Scotia it's called Heritage Day, and in P.E.I. it's known as Islander Day.) This is basically a way to give Canadians a day off in February, when it's likely cold and miserable and everyone just needs a break. Unless you live in Newfoundland and Labrador, Quebec, or one of the territories. Then you're out of luck. Have fun at work.

VICTORIA DAY

The Monday Before May 25

Canada is the only country that celebrates the birthday of Queen Victoria. We're not sure why we do that, but nevertheless it's one of our favorite holidays. The holiday marks the unofficial beginning of summer and usually involves drinking, barbecuing, and, if you're lucky, spending time at a lake or park with friends and family. Because Canadians call a case of twenty-four beers a "two four" and because Victoria Day falls around the weekend of May 24, Victoria Day is often just referred to as "May two four weekend."

CANADA DAY

July 1

Canada Day celebrates the 1867 joining of Canada's various bits into a single nation called the Dominion of Canada. Although it was still a British colony after confederation, the date is now generally considered to be Canada's official birthday. The holiday is similar in tone to the Fourth of July in the United States—there are fireworks, barbequing, beer, and patriotism galore. Canucks don maple leaf–themed gear and gather in backyards and public parks across the land to celebrate. The nation's capital of Ottawa puts on a massive celebration on Parliament Hill that's worth attending once in your life.

THANKSGIVING DAY

Second Monday in October

Thanksgiving has been an official holiday in Canada since 1957, although the practice of celebrating with a harvest festival goes back to as early as the 1500s, according to some historians. In practice it looks the same as American Thanksgiving, with families getting together to eat turkey, stuffing, and cranberry sauce. And although the holiday is celebrated here, it's nowhere near as popular as it is in the United States. For example, it's not a federal holiday, which means depending on which province you're in, you may not even get the day off.

REMEMBRANCE DAY

November 11

Similar to American Memorial Day, Remembrance Day is when Canadians remember their war dead. It's held on November 11, the day World War I ended. At the eleventh minute of the eleventh hour Canada observes a minute of silence. Taps is played, and usually there's a reading of John McCrae's poem "In Flanders Fields." The Canadian physician and lieutenant colonel wrote the poem in honor of one of his friends who was killed in World War I; most Canadian schoolchildren have to memorize this poem at some point. In the week or two leading up to Remembrance Day, some Canadians choose to wear a red poppy pin to symbolize the poppies in the poem. The holiday is generally not seen as political—observing the day is not viewed as supporting current military efforts—but rather as a way to honor and remember those who died.

"We are now emerging into an age when different civilizations will have to learn to live side by side in peaceful interchange, learning from each other, studying each other's history and ideals, art, and culture, mutually enriching each other's lives. The only alternative in this overcrowded little world is misunderstanding, tension, clash, and—catastrophe."

—Prime Minister Lester B. Pearson

"In Flanders Field" by John McCrae

In Flanders fields the poppies blow

Between the crosses, row on row,

That mark our place; and in the sky

The larks, still bravely singing, fly

Scarce heard amid the guns below.

We are the Dead. Short days ago

We lived, felt dawn, saw sunset glow,

Loved and were loved, and now we lie,

In Flanders fields.

Take up our quarrel with the foe:

To you from failing hands we throw

The torch; be yours to hold it high.

If ye break faith with us who die

We shall not sleep,

　　though poppies grow

In Flanders fields.

Remembrance Day

Poppy pin

BOXING DAY

December 26

The day after Christmas is like a Canadian Black Friday: everyone goes shopping. If you ask a random Canadian what this holiday is all about, they might be able to tell you it's a British tradition or that it may be a reference to the leftover boxes you have after the holidays. But we don't think too hard about it—it's a shopping holiday.

A NEW HOLIDAY IN THE WORKS

There is also a proposed statutory holiday in the works that would serve to acknowledge the history of residential schools in Canada. See page 82 for an explanation on the residential school system that forcibly placed Indigenous kids in boarding schools. Proposed dates are June 21, which is currently National Indigenous People's Day, and September 30, currently Orange Shirt Day, which pays respect to residential school survivors.

beaver

Montreal
bagel

snowmobile

od
ongues

Vietnamese
Pho
???

Keanu on skates

The
qu

Justin
Trudeau +
ieber)

The Sourtoe

pouti

'''s

Bear
spar

French stop sign

ARRÊT

maple
leaf

acorn

to

double
double

pine trees

rye whisky

eat
me

CN Tower
(not to
scale)

Pizza
Pizza

garlic
dipping
sauce

moose burg

hockey

loon

Kiss the cod

1$

???

Bo

anne
with
an "e"

kilometres

canoe

loonie

IMMIGRATING TO CANADA

It Seems Like a Lot of Paperwork, but I'm Up for It. Now What? Which Path Is Best for Me?

"There are no limits to the majestic future which lies before the mighty expanse of Canada with its virile, aspiring, cultured, and generous-hearted people."

—Sir Winston Churchill

FINDING YOUR WAY IN

Immigrating to Canada requires a lot of time, effort, and a bit of money. The paperwork can feel endless, and it's tough to know where to start. Luckily this section will break down a few of the most common options and explain what to expect.

PERMANENT RESIDENCY

If you want to live, work, and study anywhere in Canada, your best bet is to become a permanent resident. The benefits are similar to having a Green Card in the United States. Study permits and work permits are also an option if you're looking for a more temporary move, which we'll also explore.

Becoming a permanent resident comes with a catch, however. Once you're approved, you must still fulfill the Canadian residency requirement to maintain your status: you must live in Canada for at least 730 days (two years) out of every five years. Once you've fulfilled this residency requirement, you can also apply for Canadian citizenship. Or you can stay a permanent resident indefinitely as long as you follow the rules. Got it?

The first step is figuring out which path to permanent residency you want to take. There are two main paths to choose from and two options that may allow you to apply for permanent residency at a later date. Although there are other ways to enter Canada—perhaps you're a Ghanaian billionaire who'd like to move to Canada and invest your money building a new factory in Saskatchewan. Guess what? It's fairly easy for people like you to immigrate!—the rest of us schmucks must enter the country like normal human beings with average-sized bank accounts. So here are the most likely avenues on offer to regular people.

1) **Apply for Express Entry as a skilled immigrant.**

2) **Get sponsored by a Canadian spouse or family member.**

And here are some alternate routes to legally living in Canada without first applying for permanent residency.

3) **Enroll as a student at a Canadian university or college.** This path requires a study permit. You may be eligible to extend your study permit and at a later date to apply for permanent residency.

4) **Have a job offer in hand.** This path requires a work permit. You may be eligible at a later date to apply for permanent residency.

If it's not obvious to you which option is going to work best for you, here are a few questions to help you think about it.

Do you have a job offer in Canada? Check with human resources about the next step. If they're not handling the application for you, you'll need to apply for a work permit.

Are you in high school and looking for an affordable place to go to college? Apply to Canadian colleges and universities and come with a study permit.

Do you have a Canadian spouse that would sponsor you? Apply to be sponsored by a spouse.

Can you find one?

Kidding.

Do you have family in Canada who would sponsor you? Apply to be sponsored by a family member.

Do you have the experience or education that would qualify you to come to Canada as a skilled immigrant? Apply for Express Entry.

Are you a billionaire? Get your butler to figure out where to send the wire transfer.

YOUR PAPERS, PLEASE

No matter which route you take to apply for entry into Canada, you'll be required to provide a boatload of paperwork to support your application. So, take a moment to locate and organize important papers, request ones from relevant agencies that you don't have on hand, and make copies of the ones you'll need to submit. If you've had legal issues in the past, be aware that will come up during the application process and you may need to provide additional documentation to explain any such issues. Keep in mind that a police certificate can take ages to get once you've submitted your request to the relevant police department. Plan to ask for it as soon as you've begun the application process.

Depending on what kind of application you choose to submit, you may be asked to provide any of the following:

○ Bank statements

○ Birth certificate

○ Current résumé

○ Additional evidence providing proof of a real relationship (love letters, emails, social media posts, photographs, evidence of joint finances, etc.) if applying to be sponsored by a spouse

(continued on next page)

- O FBI background check
- O Language proficiency test results
- O Letter of acceptance from a Canadian college or university
- O Marriage certificate
- O Medical records
- O Passport
- O Police certificate
- O Proof of a job offer
- O Proof of education
- O Tax returns for the last three years

Possible barriers to immigration that may require additional documentation and may negatively affect or delay your application include:

- O Criminal record
- O Missing documents or an incomplete application
- O Unclear family situation, such as a pending divorce, adoption, or custody dispute
- O Untruthful or unverifiable statements during the application process

❶ APPLY FOR EXPRESS ENTRY AS A SKILLED IMMIGRANT

Average wait time: six months

One common way to begin a life in Canada is to come as a skilled immigrant via the Express Entry Program. In 80 percent of cases, an Express Entry application is approved in less than six months. The main advantage to the Express Entry Program, apart from its speediness, is that everything can be done online—all necessary documents can be scanned and uploaded, and fees can be paid via secure online payment methods. It also doesn't require you to have existing contacts or family in Canada. You also don't need to have a job offer in order to apply. In fact, according to Immigration, Refugees and Citizenship Canada (IRCC), 90 percent of Express Entry candidates who received an Invitation to Apply (ITA) for permanent residence in the first half of 2017 did not have a job offer.

This path is for professionals who have education and experience in their chosen field. It's also meant to bring in workers who can fill gaps in the existing job market—people who work in fields in which there aren't enough Canadians to fill necessary roles. These days that often means people who work in finance, engineering, tech, architecture, government administration, or medicine as well as workers skilled in trades like welding and carpentry. It usually doesn't apply to careers like teaching, where there are loads of qualified Canadians ready to fill those positions.

The steps for Express Entry are:

1) Head to the Government of Canada website (canada.ca) and search for "express entry." Fill out a quick form to determine whether you're eligible to apply. Gather the required documents.

2) Submit an Express Entry profile online and have it accepted. You'll be assigned a score (more on this later) based on your application. If your score is high enough, you'll get an invitation to apply for permanent residence.

3) Fill out your permanent residency application within sixty days of being invited to apply.

Express Entry applications are assigned a Comprehensive Ranking System (CRS) score out of 1,200. Points are given for skills and experience, education, proficiency in English, and even the language skills of your partner and family members. Additional points are assigned if you're fluent in French or have a Canadian degree, an immediate family member who is already a citizen, or a valid job offer. There's a quiz on the government of Canada website that lets you see in advance how many points you might earn if you were to apply.

JUST STOPPING BY?

Americans and EU nationals can visit Canada for up to six months without a visa. You can apply for an extension, but this is granted at the discretion of border control personnel (read: it's risky to bank on). If you're just looking for an extended vacation to Canada, visiting for a few months as a tourist may be your best bet. Make sure to have a return ticket in hand to show border control—officers may ask for evidence that you actually plan on heading back to the States once your trip is done. Note that you can't work while you're here on vacation. If you're planning to work in Canada or want to stay longer than six months, you'll need to figure out which path you want to take to do that legally.

❷ GET SPONSORED BY A FAMILY MEMBER OR SPOUSE

Average processing time: twelve months

This is another common path to permanent residency in Canada if you've already got family members who are citizens or permanent residents or if you're married to a Canadian citizen or permanent resident. This option takes a bit longer than the other options due to the additional paperwork involved and the high number of applicants. In the case of a spousal sponsorship, it requires a lot of supplemental information to prove you're both in love and not trying to cheat the system. Be prepared to deliver social media evidence of your relationship, a list of people who attended your wedding, and the dates when you met each other's friends and families. There will also likely be an in-person interview with a Canadian immigration officer. (Sound familiar? That's because it's the plot of *The Proposal* with Sandra Bullock and Ryan Reynolds.)

1) Find out if your spouse or relative is eligible to sponsor you. For starters, they must be a Canadian citizen or a permanent resident living in Canada.

2) Both parties need to gather the necessary documents (see list of potential documents you'll need to gather on pages 55-56 or find the checklist online at canada.ca) and send in their required parts of the application. Sponsors need to prove they've got enough money in the bank to support the applicant if needed, for example. Applicants need to prove they aren't violent criminals and such.

3) Once the application for sponsorship is being processed, a case officer will contact you and alert you to any additional document requests as well as arrange to schedule your interview.

4) Once the application is accepted, the applicant will have a limited amount of time to enter Canada and begin life as a permanent resident.

❸ ENROLLING AS A STUDENT AT A CANADIAN UNIVERSITY OR COLLEGE

Average processing time: two weeks

Congrats on your choice to get an education in Canada! The schools are top notch, and the degree won't put you in debt for life—or, at least, not as much debt as a US education requires. International tuition fees for a bachelor of arts at McGill University, for example, are about $16,000 Canadian per year. Compare that with the University of Michigan's out-of-state fees of nearly $50,000 US. It's insane. It's a wonder Canadian schools aren't more packed with Americans trying to save money.

Anyway, once you've been accepted to a program in Canada, you'll need to apply for a student visa online and pay a fee. This will be valid for the length of your study program and a few weeks afterward.

❹ HAVING A JOB OFFER IN HAND

Average processing time: two weeks

Keep in mind that hiring someone from outside Canada requires a lot of paperwork and certifications and that most employers aren't going to bother. So if the plan is to just apply for Canadian jobs while living in the United States, you might find yourself out of luck. Big corporations or large institutions like banks are probably more likely to offer jobs to non-Canadians because their recruiters and human resource departments are familiar with the process and will be able to undertake the necessary steps at their end—and these likely won't be entry-level positions but rather managerial or professional ones.

But if you do get an offer, congrats! If you've got the right experience that Canadian employers are looking for, this is one of the easiest ways to move to Canada. Once you have a valid offer, you'll need to apply for an employer-specific work permit. This can be done online with the help of your employer. Once you're granted a work permit, you're allowed to work for that specific employer; if you leave the position or are fired, the permit is no longer valid.

BEWARE OF FRAUD: CANADIANS CAN BE CROOKS TOO

Keep in mind that whatever path you choose will cost you money. There are basic application and processing fees payable to government agencies at every step. Educate yourself about what kind of legitimate fees to expect from the official Canadian government website, www.canada.ca. There may also be fees associated with getting your FBI background check, for example, as well as fees to send your documents by certified mail.

If you choose to hire an accredited immigration professional to help with the process, you're likely looking at a few extra thousand dollars on top of the government fees. Please keep in mind that there are hundreds of organizations out there offering Canadian immigration services. It can be confusing figuring out what's worth your time—every year people swindle hopeful immigrants by taking advantage of them. Do your research before engaging any of these services. Look for companies or counsel that employs professional attorneys of good standing and have a track record of submitting successful immigration applications.

KNOW YOUR RIGHTS

All right, so you're coming to Canada one way or another and want to know exactly what you're entitled to while you're here. Big surprise. Check out this handy section to see what to expect when you're here under various circumstances.

TOURIST

I'm here to see Niagara Falls!

Right to work: No

Free health care: No

Right to vote: No

Eligible for driver's license: No. Tourists can drive with a valid driver's license from their own country for up to ninety days.

Eligible for social insurance number (see page 69): No

Eligible for a Canadian passport: No, dummy.

Run for office: LOL

INTERNATIONAL STUDENT
(Temporary Resident)

I'm here to study law and also hopefully party a lot. Probably at Western.[8]

Right to work: Depends on your study visa, but generally yes with conditions

Free health care: Depends on the province. For example, B.C. and Alberta offer free health coverage to students, while Ontario and Quebec require students to pay for their own.

Right to vote: No

Eligible for driver's license: Yes. License holders from certain countries like the US and the UK can exchange a valid license for a Canadian one after taking an eye test and providing another form of ID like a passport.

Eligible for social insurance number: Depends on your study visa, but generally yes

Eligible for a Canadian passport: No

Run for office: No

---

8   I'm sure it's a fine school and that people learn things there.

REFUGEE CLAIMANT[9]

I risked everything to get here.

This is someone whose claim hasn't yet been approved. Once a refugee claim has been approved, the applicant becomes a permanent resident.

Right to work: Yes, with a valid work permit.

Free health care: Yes, under the Interim Federal Health Programme (IFHP) until refugee claim is accepted, after which the provincial system will cover them. If the claim is rejected, coverage extends until deportation.

Right to vote: No

Eligible for driver's license: Yes. In the event they don't have an international driving permit already from their home country, they'll need to enroll in driver education classes and apply for a license.

Eligible for social insurance number: Yes, with a valid work permit

Eligible for a Canadian passport: No

Run for office: No

---

9   Odds are next to nothing that, say, American citizens would be approved refugee status in Canada. This is for people fleeing war and persecution and who will likely die if they remain in their home country. The parameters for who qualifies as a refugee are laid out in the United Nations 1951 Refugee Convention.

PERMANENT RESIDENT

I've jumped through all (or most of) the hoops. Give me my benefits already.

Right to work: Yes

Free health care: Yes

Right to vote: No

Eligible for driver's license: Yes. Americans can exchange a valid US license for a Canadian one after taking an eye test and providing another form of ID like a passport.

Eligible for social insurance number: Yes

Eligible for a Canadian passport: No

Run for office: No

maple syrup ration

Welcome!
(not really)

CITIZEN

I'm Canadian, and it's glorious.

Right to work: Yes

Free health care: Yes

Right to vote: Yes

Eligible for driver's license: Yes. Americans can exchange a valid US license for a Canadian one after taking an eye test and providing another form of ID like a passport.

Eligible for social insurance number: Yes

Eligible for a Canadian passport: Yes

Run for office: Yes

YOU'RE A PERMANENT RESIDENT—NOW WHAT?

"A Canadian is merely an unarmed American with health care."

—John Wing

Congratulations! Your application has been processed and accepted. By now you should have also received your PR card in the mail. This allows you to apply for a health card and a social insurance number. So let's get you set up with the essential pieces of government ID you'll need for a life here.

SOCIAL INSURANCE CARD

Your social insurance number (SIN) is similar to your social security number in the United States. To work in Canada or access government programs like health care, you need a social insurance number. Luckily, applying is easy. Find your local Service Canada office and bring the necessary original documents with you—basically stuff like your birth certificate, permanent residence card, and work visa. You'll get your number on the spot. If you're too far from a Service Canada office, you can also apply by mail.

OPENING A BANK ACCOUNT

Regardless of how long you plan to stay, it's a good idea to open a Canadian bank account. This allows you to get direct deposits from your employer, use bank machines without paying foreign transaction fees, and, eventually, apply for mortgages and car loans.

The good news is that because Canada welcomes so many new immigrants, banks have adapted to make things easy on these new arrivals. Many of them have packages specially designed for new immigrants, so do your research and find the one that best matches your needs. The Royal Bank of Canada (RBC) has a "Welcome to Canada" package, while Scotia Bank offers the "Start Right" program.

To open an account you will need to go in person to your chosen bank branch and bring two pieces of government-issued ID. Your permanent resident card, social insurance card, and health card should be sufficient. Check with the individual branch before you go, however, to ensure you've got the right documents.

One thing that's a bit of a bummer for Americans is that credit history doesn't carry over from country to country—or perhaps that's good news for you. Even if you bank with TD Bank in the United States, for example, TD Canada will have no record of your credit history. (This is a lesson I learned the hard way when I went the other way. My high Canadian credit score was useless in the United States, and my beloved TD wouldn't approve me for an American credit card. I ended up with a weird Florida one that had a picture of a sports car on it and a $500 spending limit.) Anyway, the banking packages geared toward immigrants also usually include a credit card. Start using it right away to build credit, and always pay off your bill every month.

HEALTH CARD

This card is your access to Canada's health care system. Once you're eligible for it, you'll need to ensure you've got your SIN number first. Find your local government issuing office by searching for the nearest location online, and bring the necessary original documents with you—among other documents, you'll definitely need your SIN number, permanent residence card, proof of residency in the province or territory of application, and proof of identity (passport or birth certificate). Check online to make sure you've got all the paperwork before you go in person. There's nothing more frustrating than showing up and not having the right documents.

Once you get your card in the mail, you need to keep it with you always. When you go to the doctor or to the hospital, the person checking you in will ask to see the card. Show it to them. That's it. No paperwork. No bills a few weeks later in the mail. No copay. Civilized, isn't it?

DRIVER'S LICENSE

As a resident, your US license is only good in Canada for sixty days, so you'll need to swap it out for a Canadian one. Thankfully it's a very painless process. Head to your local government office[10]—they've got names like ServiceOntario—and bring original ID showing your name, date of birth, and signature along with your valid US driver's license and any supporting documents you may need. They may also ask for proof of your driving experience, so you may need letters from your car insurance company or the DMV in your home state. Fill out an application and pay the administration fee, and they'll administer an eye test. Once the license arrives, remember to always have it with you while driving, or else you risk getting a ticket.

---

10 Unlike many places in the United States, the offices here that provide driver's licenses are normal, civilized institutions run efficiently by human beings who don't hate you. I once got my driver's license and health card renewed at the same location in the amount of time it took my friend to go next door and buy us both coffee. It was maybe ten minutes. You can actually renew them online now, so today you don't even need to get dressed to enjoy these government services.

Quiz: Find Your Canadian City Soulmate

When it comes to Canadian cities, not all are created equal. Find out which one is the best match for you! Of course, there are thousands of great spots all over the country that would make a great place to call home—so don't get too hung up on the results. Even though they're 100 percent accurate.

1 When it comes to booze, you prefer:

    A. A dive bar with live music and local ale on tap

    B. A British-style brewpub with a view of the water

    C. A rooftop hotel bar overlooking the city skyline and a vodka cocktail made with burnt sage and rosemary bitters

    D. Somewhere with fiddle music and a good selection of strong rum

    E. A saloon with a pool table and cheap drink specials on karaoke night

    F. A cozy nook with a fireplace, rabbit poutine, and a glass of chianti

2 What would be your dream midnight snack?

    A.   A plate of pierogis and kielbasa

    B.   Sushi

    C.   A fish taco, some fried chicken, and Dim Sum

    D.   Fish and chips

    E.   A buffalo burger with mushrooms

    F.   A smoked meat sandwich with a deli pickle

3 If you could identify one issue you're most passionate about it would be:

    A.   A fair justice system

    B.   Environmentalism

    C.   Affordable housing

    D.   Job creation

    E.   Climate change

    F.   Anything to do with local politics

4 When it comes to exercise, you prefer:

A. Biking in a few feet of snow

B. A day out on the water with a stand-up paddleboard

C. A candlelit hip-hop spin class

D. Hiking up a big windy hill for a view of the ocean or some moose hunting

E. Snowshoeing, cross-country skiing, and ice fishing

F. Wine drinking

5 Your favorite color is:

A. Prairie wheat

B. Treetop green

C. Smog gray

D. Ocean blue

E. Actual gold

F. Snow white

6 When it comes to meeting people, you'd most likely be drawn to:

A. A bass player who also does art installations

B. Someone you met in yoga class

C. A fellow cyclist you met at a rally for more bike lanes

D. An oil painter who used to work on a sailing ship

E. Someone who flies propeller planes for a living

F. A photography student who has a part-time job at a bagel shop down the road

RESULTS:

Mostly As: Winnipeg

Mostly Bs: Vancouver

Mostly Cs: Toronto

Mostly Ds: St. John's

Mostly Es: Whitehorse

Mostly Fs: Montreal

od
ongues

beaver

Montreal
bagel

snowmobile

The
qu

Vietnamese
Pho

Keanu on skates

The Sourtoe

pout

Justin
Trudeau +
ieber)

Bear
spar

French stop sign

ARRÊT

maple
leaf

acorn

toa

double
double

pine trees

rye whisky

eat
me

CN Tower
(not to
scale)

Pizza
Pizza

garlic
dipping
sauce

moose burg

hockey

Kiss the cod

1$

loon

anne
with
an "e"

kilometres

canoe

loonie

Bo

ACCLIMATING TO CANADIAN CULTURE

Jargon to Learn, Weird Foods to Eat, and People to Know. Also, Tips on How to Act Around Canadians (No Sudden Movements)

"Americans are benevolently ignorant about Canada, while Canadians are malevolently well informed about the United States."

—J. Bartlet Brebner

THINGS THAT MAY SURPRISE YOU

There's a tendency to assume that because Canada is so similar to the United States, with a shared language and similar customs, that there isn't *that* much to learn about Canada. But there are some weird things that Americans will be surprised to find out—things you assume are part of our shared history (like war in Vietnam, for example) that are simply alien to most Canucks. And, of course, there are everyday things that will surprise you, too.

WE LOVE CUBA

"Sexiest man I've ever met."

—Margaret Trudeau,
wife of Pierre Trudeau and mother of
Justin Trudeau, on Fidel Castro

Fun fact: Cuban president Fidel Castro was a pallbearer at former prime minister Pierre Trudeau's funeral, along with Jimmy Carter and Leonard Cohen. Unlike the United States,

Canada never had any issues with Cuba, and our governments have always managed to get along. What that means for Canadians, practically, is that you can vacation in sunny Cuba any time (without running into any Americans). This is a surprising incentive for many, and about a million Canadians visit the country every year. Which leads us to . . .

CANADIANS HAVE SOME PREJUDICES AGAINST THE UNITED STATES

"I want to thank all the Canadians who came out today to wave to me—with all five fingers!"

—George W. Bush, during his first visit to Ottawa, 2004

Canadians have a reputation for being nice. And it's true: we're often nice to your face. But we're also a bit smug and superior, especially when it comes to the United States. Just like the Scots have a particular view of the English and New Zealanders of Australians, when it comes to the United States, many Canadians have strong and often negative opinions. For example, we have very strong opinions on your presidents. Stay here long enough, and you'll probably hear snide comments about the state of the American public education system, the lack of affordable health care, the racism, and the ignorance about other cultures (which generally means ignorance about Canada. We're a sensitive bunch). Despite this general feeling of smug superiority, Canadians know that the health and prosperity of our nation is tied to that of the United States and that it's better for everyone if we get along. Plus, Canadians love warm American weather. Throw a rock in Myrtle Beach, Palm Springs, or Key West, and you'll hit a Canadian on vacation—who will apologize for getting in the way of your rock.

CANADIANS ARE RACIST, TOO

Look, Canada is great, but it isn't a paradise wonderland without its own set of serious issues. This isn't knocking the fact that there are millions of lovely, kind people in this country who welcome newcomers and hold reasonable views about most things. But just like any other country in the world and despite our reputation for tolerance and openness, you will unfortunately find both systemic and regular, old-guy-on-the-street racism here. The systemic racism is mainly a result of the Canadian government's residential school system, which took Indigenous children from their families and placed them in boarding schools, where they often endured horrific abuse. The goal of these schools, where more than 150,000 children were forced to attend, was "kill the Indian in the child." Canada is still coming to terms with the legacy of these schools that has deeply affected generations of Indigenous families. Canada has also had discriminatory policies and laws targeting Chinese, Japanese, and black Canadians.

Though it's not common, if you or someone you know is the unfortunate target of any kind of racism, know that there are harassment and hate crime laws in place to protect you and that the police and the courts are getting better about taking these things seriously.

WINTER IS COLD

"Unconsciously, Canadians feel that any people can live where the climate is gentle. It takes a special people to prosper where nature makes it so hard."

—Robert MacNeil, journalist

Unless you're from an area of the world that gets a lot of snow—Minnesota, Upstate New York, or Michigan, for example—the Canadian winters are going to come as a shock. Temperatures can dip to -30 degrees Celsius or colder across most of the country. Places like Toronto get a yearly average of almost 50 inches of snow, while the town of St. Antony in Newfoundland and Labrador gets around 214 inches. In fact, the only part of Canada where you *won't* experience freezing temperatures and lots of the white stuff are some parts of British Columbia; there you can expect just cold, wet rain, and sleet. Basically, no matter where you're living, it's going to be slushy, wet, and cold for a good six to eight months of the year, so be prepared to invest in a good-quality winter coat and boots. Also, a hat and gloves. And a shovel or snow blower for your driveway. And an ice scraper for your car. Driving in snow will take some getting used to as well. On a more positive note, now's your chance to take up a winter sport. Check out your local curling club, try your hand at cross-country skiing, or just head out to the slopes with your toboggan and embrace the cold. Be sure to have some hot chocolate on hand for later, though.

"There are few, if any, Canadian men that have never spelled their name in a snowbank."

—Douglas Coupland

CANADA DIDN'T PARTICIPATE IN THE VIETNAM WAR

Although Canada wasn't officially part of the war in Vietnam, many Canadians volunteered to serve in the US forces. (It goes both ways: before the United States entered the First and Second World Wars, many Americans went north to enlist in the Canadian forces.) It's estimated that around 12,000 Canadians fought in Vietnam, with 134 Canadian citizens killed or declared missing in the war.

American draft dodgers—also known as conscientious objectors—and deserters came to Canada by the thousands. Immigration records show that around 20,000 to 30,000 draft-age American men fled north, while some estimates put the number as high as 125,000. They were mostly middle-class, college-educated, left-leaning guys who didn't particularly care to go to fight in a war they didn't support. Most of them fit right in and became productive members of Canadian society.

After the war around eleven thousand Vietnamese refugees, also known as "the boat people," came to Canada—way more than immigrated to any other country. They settled in cities like Toronto, Montreal, and Vancouver and have greatly contributed to Canadian culture—delicious Vietnamese restaurants are just one

Vietnamese Pho

of their contributions. In fact, in a beautiful pay-it-forward gesture, many Vietnamese families who were welcomed as refugees in the 1970s banded together to help sponsor Syrian refugee families resettling in Canada.

Former Vietnamese refugee Tom Tang, in an interview with the *Globe and Mail*, noted, "We were in the Syrians' shoes back then and I think because the Vietnamese community has more-or-less been a successful integration that we need to come forward to show Canadians, our country, that taking in refugees is a good thing—we became tax paying citizens, we give back to the country."

WE DIDN'T GO TO WAR WITH IRAQ, EITHER

Canada aided the Iraq War in numerous ways—such as postinvasion training for the Iraqi military, ship deployments in the region, Canadian troops serving in the US military, and so on—but it wasn't officially part of the "Coalition of the Willing." Prime Minister Jean Chrétien refused to send troops unless the mission had the approval of the United Nations, which it famously did not. This was okay with most Canadians, who believed the war was misguided and unnecessary. Canada did send troops to Afghanistan after 9/11, though.

OUR TAXES ARE HIGHER

Yeah, this may not be a surprise. You know Canada has higher taxes compared to the United States, and that's why we have accessible health care; subsidized day care; quality roads, schools, and police services; and a generally higher quality of living. But practically, on a day-to-day level, paying something like sales tax takes some getting used to.

Canada's federal sales tax is called the Goods and Services Tax (GST, or PST in Quebec) and is set at 5 percent. Many provinces have combined their own additional sales tax with the federal tax, and that is called the Harmonized Sales Tax (HST). The province of Alberta and the three territories do not have their own taxes. In Ontario the HST is 13 percent, and in the Atlantic provinces it's 15 percent. A shirt with a price tag of $29.99 is going to ring up as $33 in Ontario and $33.50 in P.E.I., for example. However, necessities like groceries and prescription drugs are tax-free. You'll also be paying higher taxes on your personal income, but your accountant can explain all that to you. If it helps, just think of each bit of tax you pay as a tiny investment in a better society— or a deposit on your "free" bypass surgery a few years down the line.

ONLINE SHOPPING KIND OF SUCKS HERE

Online shopping is a way of life in the United States (as is crippling credit card debt, for some reason). But shopping online in Canada isn't quite as popular for several reasons, so get ready to patronize your local brick-and-mortar stores, unless you're some kind of millionaire. The issue with online shopping in Canada is that many companies are based in the United States and charge exorbitant shipping fees to Canada. Some companies don't ship to Canada at all, while others, such as Amazon, offer limited selection compared to their American sites. If you must get your online shopping fix, check out some made-in-Canada retailers like Roots, Sorel, Hudson's Bay, or Aritzia, or find a US company that has a dedicated Canadian site.

Here are a few things to keep in mind before you click "confirm order."

Shipping charges. It's a big country. It costs a lot of money to have something shipped to Whitehorse or Gander from a shipping distribution center in Texas. Some companies won't ship to Canada at all.

Taxes and duty. Whatever you import to Canada is subject to Canadian import charges. The buyer is responsible for paying these fees. You may find a deal on a new lamp for $20 but end up owing $30 in taxes and duty by the time it gets to your house. So be forewarned.

Shipping delays. Because your parcel needs to be processed by Canadian customs, it's nearly impossible to determine exactly when you'll get your stuff. Packages can be held up in customs for days or even weeks. So, if you're buying a made-in-China T-shirt with a beaver on it from an American seller on eBay and need it in time for Canada Day, you better plan ahead and order early.

The exchange rate. If you're buying from a US site, keep in mind that those prices are in US dollars. Depending on the exchange rate, it may not be as much of a deal as it looks like.

CELL PHONE SERVICE IS SUPER EXPENSIVE

Get ready for sticker shock when it comes to buying and operating a cell phone in Canada: Canadians pay some of the highest rates in the world. In a 2016 study commissioned by the Canadian Radio-Television and Telecommunications Commission, Canada ranked highest or second highest for wireless pricing among the eight nations surveyed. Not only does the physical phone cost more than it does in other countries, you pay more for data, roaming, and basic services. (Unlike the United States, where the entire country is covered, some Canadian providers even charge roaming fees inside the country.)

One of the explanations for the higher cost is that due to the size of the country and its relatively sparse population outside of cities, it becomes expensive for providers to install the necessary infrastructure to support affordable service everywhere. You can find affordable plans, but you don't get much for your money: for example, one major provider offers a $25 monthly plan that gets you 150 local minutes, 50 text messages, and no data. They might consider calling that one the "It's the year 2004" plan. So be prepared to research your options and only pay for what you absolutely need. And perhaps be prepared to give up the habit of streaming baby goat videos on YouTube during your morning commute.

WE HAVE CANADIAN CONTENT LAWS TO PROTECT THE CULTURE

It isn't your imagination—you are hearing a lot of Avril Lavigne, Alanis Morissette, and other Canadian artists on the radio here in Canada. Turn on the TV or browse Netflix, and you'll also notice a boatload of Canadian TV shows and films shot in Canada and starring Canadian artists. This is due to Canadian content (CanCon) laws that require a certain amount of whatever you see or hear to be written, produced, acted, and/or sung by a Canadian. These laws were enacted in the late sixties and early seventies to ensure that

American and British media wouldn't subsume our burgeoning Canadian culture. For Canadian culture and identity to thrive, the belief went, Canadians needed to see and hear themselves on TV, in films, and on the radio. (Around this time we also began to see the birth of Canadian literature, thanks to authors like Margaret Atwood and Leonard Cohen.) Generally, for the radio, 40 percent of all content must be Canadian, while for broadcasting it's 60 percent. Although not without controversy at the time, these laws are likely the reason classic hit shows like *Degrassi*, *Second City Television*, *Today's Special*, *Trailer Park Boys*, and *Mr. Dressup* were able to find both funding and an audience.

It's also why you can't escape that particular brand of bad (but lovable) Canadian pop music during your morning commute.

Some radio stations were so irritated at being forced to play what they considered lame Canadian music—keep in mind this was the era of the Beatles and Elvis—that they began playing all the Canadian content in the middle of the night, leaving peak hours for the real hits. Those after-dark blocks jokingly became known as "beaver hour."

How do you figure out if a song is Canadian or not? Consult the MAPL system. (I'm not sure if they were going for MAPLE here, but you'd think they could have come up with something beginning with E to make the acronym make more sense.) Nevertheless. For a song to be Canadian, it must meet two of the following requirements:

M (music): The music is composed entirely by a Canadian.

A (artist): The music or the lyrics are performed by a Canadian.

P (performance): The musical selection consists of a performance that is either (a) recorded wholly in Canada, or (b) performed wholly in Canada and broadcast live in Canada.

L (lyrics): The lyrics are written entirely by a Canadian.

Céline

So even if, for example, a famous Canadian artist like Justin Bieber sings every song on his album, the work may not qualify as Canadian content unless it meets one of the other MAPL requirements. So enjoy what the country has to offer. Don't fight it. Lean into the magic. Start with the *Road to Avonlea* series, then listen to an Anne Murray album. Or if your tastes are more modern, start with the *Alias Grace* series, then listen to some Donovan Woods.

"Canada didn't have MTV. They had something called MUCH Music with their own veejays and stuff. They don't get references to Kurt Loder or Martha Quinn."

—Kyle M., Toronto via Orange County

WEIRD AND IMPORTANT THINGS INVENTED BY CANADIANS

Canadians like to invent stuff. Perhaps it's because we have a lot of time to sit indoors and think during the long winters. Perhaps we're a country of truly stable geniuses. Who's to say? The fact is Canucks have invented quite a bit of useful things over the years. And just like we love to tell you which of your favorite actors are actually Canadian, we love to tell you about all the random shit we invented—whose origins no one has ever once stopped to wonder about.

- **Basketball** (invented by a Canadian living in Massachusetts)

- **Egg cartons**

- **Electric wheelchairs**

- **Five-pin bowling** (great for kids and weaklings)

- **Garbage bags**

- **Goalie masks**

- **Hawaiian pizza** (you're welcome)

- **IMAX**

- **Insulin** (all right, Canadians Frederick Banting and Charles Best discovered this rather than invented it, but still . . .)

- **JavaScript**

(continued on next page)

- **Jet skis**

- **Lacrosse**

- **Pablum baby food** (invented in the 1930s by two Canadian doctors; a hospital in Toronto still gets the royalties)

- **Pacemakers**

- **Paint rollers**

- **Peanut butter**

- **Snowmobiles**

- **Snow plows**

- **The telephone** (Alexander Graham Bell was born in Scotland and living in Canada when he invented the phone. He later became American. But claiming the telephone as a Canadian invention seems important to people, so here it is.)

- **Trivial Pursuit**

- **Yahtzee**

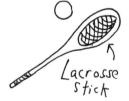

Lacrosse stick

snowmobile

"I worked at an amusement park in the U.S. over the summer, and one of my American coworkers asked if we had roller coasters in Canada. Don't be that person."

—Amanda S., Windsor

TIPS FOR YOUR FIRST CANADIAN ENCOUNTER

"Canadians have an abiding interest in surprising those Americans who have historically made little effort to learn about their neighbour to the North."

—Peter Jennings

So you've moved to Canada and your likely next step is making friends. Canadians have a high tolerance for pretty much anything except rudeness. Unfortunately, many Canadians have been brought up believing in the ugly American stereotype—rude, loud, pushy, gun-loving, and a bit ignorant. Presumably you're moving to Canada because you're an enlightened person who respects other cultures, so *you* won't have to worry about this. But just in case, to smooth over your first interactions with real Canadians, here are a few things you'll want to keep in mind.

Do not make Canada jokes. Ever. Hoser, aboot, the *South Park* movie, the *Canadian Bacon* movie, America's hat, "eh." These things may seem funny and innocent to you, but every Canadian has heard these jokes forty-five times, and if you do this, they will think you're boring and ignorant. But you won't know this because they will be polite to your face.

Experiment with some witty and self-deprecating humour. Yes, that's humour with a U. Try making an informed joke about Trudeau's socks or, better yet, make a joke at your own expense. "Yes, I'm American, but don't worry—I didn't bring my guns with me." Or if you're English, "Sorry about the monarchy still being a thing, but at least we gave you Harry and Meghan!" Canadians love shit like that.

Avoid making broad assumptions or statements that demonstrate you don't know anything about Canada. If someone says they're from Halifax, don't ask if that's in Quebec or tell them you have a cat named Halibut. Tell them you've heard it's lovely and you'd like to visit. Yes, fine, maybe you're lying, but just look it up later. Pretend you're (or better yet, be) informed at a very basic level about the country you've chosen to live in. It makes for a nicer conversation for everyone involved. And that, my American friend, is above all what you're striving for: *niceness*.

"The acquisition of Canada this year, as far as the neighborhood of Quebec, will be a mere matter of marching, and will give us the experience for the attack on Halifax, the next and final expulsion of England from the American continent."

— Thomas Jefferson, before the War of 1812

CANADIAN CUISINE:
Timbits, Seal Flipper Pie, and Ketchup Chips

"The fact that over 50 per cent of the residents of Toronto are not from Canada, that is always a good thing, creatively, and for food especially. That is easily a city's biggest strength, and it is Toronto's unique strength."

—Anthony Bourdain

Canada, like the United States, has a vibrant food scene, thanks in large part to its many immigrants who have made the country their home over the years. In its major cities you'll find everything from Syrian—thanks to the more than fifty thousand Syrian refugees that settled here beginning in 2015—to Vietnamese to Caribbean to Lebanese and dozens more besides.[11] If you're looking for gluten-free, halal, kosher, or vegetarian, you should locate it easily, whether you're in Moose Jaw or Muskoka. In Charlottetown, for example, Canada's smallest provincial capital with a population of about thirty-six thousand people, you'll

---

11 One exception to this is the smaller number of Mexican restaurants you'll find in Canada compared to the United States, although this is slowly improving as demographics change. My cousin from California once laughed at me for not knowing how to properly eat a taco (apparently this involved folding the back end of the tortilla up to prevent the filling from sliding out). What did I know? The only Mexican food I'd had growing up in small town 1980s Ontario was Taco Bell.

find Afghani, Chinese, Indian, and Thai eateries within a few blocks from one another. If it's a classic burger you're after, most American chains like McDonald's and Wendy's have a presence here, too—although you'll have to do without Jack in the Box, Waffle House, Carl's Jr., In-N-Out, and White Castle. So what makes a dish *traditionally* Canadian, then? We're not sure. Try adding some gravy.

There's also a growing Indigenous food scene nationwide, with chefs creating dishes made with seal, caribou, salmon, and other local, traditionally prepared ingredients—dishes their ancestors were enjoying long before the French and English colonized the land.

poutine

The country's most well-known contribution to world cuisine is probably poutine from the province of Quebec—a messy heap of French fries layered with cheese curds and smothered in hot brown gravy. It's a million-calorie dish and tastes terrific, especially after a night of drinking. If you're so inclined, you can even buy shirts that read "Body by Poutine." In addition to fries and gravy, newcomers to Canada will find lots of unique foodstuffs to enjoy, depending on what part of the country you're in. So let's look at the Canadian treats you'll want to know about, including packaged goods like dill pickle chips as well as fresh, local cuisine like moose burgers, seal flipper pie, and tourtières.

In short, anyone moving to Canada will be relieved to find that most of their favorite foods—and food chains—are readily available. But there is also a lot to explore!

BEAVERTAILS

REGION: Ontario originally, now available throughout Canada

This long, flat pastry resembles the distinctive tail of Canada's national animal, but it tastes a lot better (or so we can assume). The name-brand treat, made of deep-fried dough and covered in cinnamon sugar, is a staple at street fairs and festivals across the country thanks to the efforts of business owners Grant and Pam Hooker. The Ontario couple turned a family recipe into a thriving international enterprise, which means you may also spot these treats at amusement parks in Utah, Colorado, or Tennessee. And if it's a celebrity endorsement you're after, President Obama was photographed enjoying a BeaverTail on his official visit to Ottawa in 2009.

BUTTER TARTS

REGION: Canada

A mini pastry shell filled with butter, eggs, brown sugar, raisins, and a dash of vanilla, this delicious dessert is found in supermarkets across the country. Bring these to a housewarming party or someone's birthday and you're sure to impress.

THE CAESAR

REGION: Alberta originally, now available throughout Canada

The hangover cure for Canadians everywhere, this classic cocktail was invented in Calgary in 1969—and we now consume 350 million of them a year. A Caesar is usually made with Clamato-brand clam juice (though the drink's inventor, Walter Chell, made the original version with a "nectar" of mashed clams), Worchestershire sauce, hot sauce, and vodka. Rim the glass with celery salt, and garnish with a celery stalk, lime wedge, and some salt and pepper. Then drink at least two. The clam juice sounds like it should be gross, but for some reason it tastes like magic.

COD TONGUE

REGION: Newfoundland and Labrador

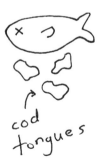

Young Newfoundlanders living near the docks used to make a few extra bucks by cutting out the tongues from the day's cod catch. The little bit of gelatinous flesh was mostly worthless to the fisherman, but the kids sold them to local shops or housewives, who fried them up with a bit of

butter and breadcrumbs. Today you'll find deep-fried cod tongues on the menu at many restaurants throughout the province.

ICE WINE

REGION: Ontario, now available throughout Canada

Ice wine is a sweet dessert wine that's made by harvesting grapes after they've frozen on the vine. This requires a climate warm enough to grow grapes but cold enough to make them freeze, which is why the Niagara region in Ontario is now the ice wine capital of the world— or would be, if there were any such competition. Canada is known around the world for its delicious high-end ice wine, so if you get the chance, give it a try.

MONTREAL-STYLE BAGELS

REGION: Montreal originally, now available throughout Canada

Montrealers and New Yorkers have a respectful rivalry when it comes to who makes the best bagels. The ones north of the border are thinner, denser, and sweeter, as the dough is boiled in honey-sweetened water before being cooked in a wood-fired oven. There's no need to forsake your New York bagel allegiance, but the Montreal bagel is a must-try nonetheless.

MONTREAL-SMOKED MEAT

REGION: Montreal originally, now available throughout Canada

Salted and cured beef brisket served on rye bread with yellow mustard—this is a Montreal institution and a must-try when visiting or living in the city. It's comparable to pastrami but with less sugar and more peppercorns and seasonings like mustard seeds and coriander. The best smoked meat to be had anywhere is probably found at Schwartz's Deli on Montreal's Saint-Laurent Boulevard (although Montrealers like to debate this). Founded in 1928 by a Romanian immigrant, the place is beloved by locals and tourists alike. Fun fact: In 1990 the Quebec-born singer Celine Dion founded a still-operational chain of restaurants called Nickels that serves smoked-meat sandwiches.

FLIPPER PIE

REGION: Newfoundland and Labrador

Flipper pie is a pot pie made with braised seal flippers, vegetables, and gravy. It's traditionally eaten in the spring, and the hearty dish is a dinnertime staple for many Newfoundlanders. Keep in mind that the seals hunted in Canada are nonendangered adult seals harvested in a sustainable and humane manner. So enjoy this unique Canadian dish because seal meat is delicious—dark and lean.

TOURTIÈRE

REGION: Quebec and the Maritimes

A hearty meat and potato pie from Quebec commonly made with pork, veal, or beef and served with fruity homemade ketchup. It can also be made with game meat or fish, depending on what's readily available. This dish is traditionally eaten on Christmas Eve or New Year's Eve in Quebec and in nearby provinces like New Brunswick, Nova Scotia, and Prince Edward Island.

MOOSE BURGERS

REGION: Newfoundland and Labrador, the Yukon

Unless you've visited Alaska, most Americans—and many Canadians—are unlikely to have sampled a moose burger. Fortunately these treats are common on the East Coast and in the northwest of Canada. Moose meat is a lean, gamey meat that works well as a burger—slap one on a bun with some lettuce and tomato, and enjoy!

SASKATOON BERRY PIE

REGION: Saskatchewan

A traditional fruit pie made with Saskatoon berries, a berry native to North America that looks like a blueberry but is more closely related to an apple. The word *Saskatoon* (also the name of a city in Saskatchewan) is thought to be derived from the Cree word *misâskwatômina*, meaning "fruit of the tree of many branches." These berries aren't the only interesting edible varieties you'll find on your travels throughout Canada; also keep an eye out for partridgeberries, cloudberries, and huckleberries—all of them perfect for pie making.

NANAIMO BARS

REGION: British Columbia originally, now available throughout Canada

Nanaimo Bar
← chocolate
Yellow frosting
crumb base

These sweet no-bake treats were voted Canada's favorite confection in a national newspaper poll. Named after a city in British Columbia, the bars consist of a chocolate-and-coconut-crumb base topped with yellow custard frosting and finished with a layer of chocolate ganache for a Canadian twist on . . . brownies, maybe? If you're ever at an event where some angel has made a plate of these, just remember to eat dessert first, as these little squares of heaven will disappear quickly. Nanaimo bars are also listed in the *Canadian Oxford Dictionary*, the only dictionary in the world where it appears (Scrabble enthusiasts take note).

SPLIT-PEA SOUP

REGION: Quebec originally, now available throughout Canada

Traditionally found in Quebec, this hearty soup made with blended peas and herbs and rounded out with bits of pork was a staple of lumberjacks who needed an affordable, calorie-rich dish to keep their energy up during the Canadian winters. Although it's still served fresh in many establishments throughout Quebec, you'll find the canned version on shelves throughout the country.

VÍNARTERTA

REGION: Manitoba

A traditional Icelandic cake that was made popular in the prairie region by Icelandic settlers in the late 1800s, vínarterta is now better known in Canada than it is back there. It's a fat layer cake made with vanilla or cardamom-flavored shortbread and spiced-plum jam. It looks like a stack of pancakes.

MAPLE TAFFY

REGION: Ontario and Quebec

Pour boiling maple syrup over a patch of fresh snow, *et voilà*, you have some sticky maple taffy, a classic—and cheap!—winter treat in Canada's maple syrup regions. A popsicle stick is used to roll up the taffy into a kind of sweet maple popsicle.

maple taffy stick

DONAIR

REGION: Nova Scotia originally, now available throughout Canada

Perfected in Halifax in the early seventies by restaurant worker Peter Gamoulakos, donairs are the Canadian version of a gyro or doner kebab. The donair comes with a sweet condensed milk sauce. It's now the city of Halifax's official food.

FIDDLEHEADS

REGION: New Brunswick and surrounding regions originally, now available throughout Canada

Traditionally harvested by Indigenous peoples on the eastern coast of Canada, this vegetable from the fern family is a popular addition to the dinner table in many Maritime households. Named after its resemblance to the curled top of the fiddle instrument, these cute little leaf buds are basically the tips of the fern's leaves before they unfurl—and they're packed with vitamin A as well as omega-3 and omega-6 fatty acids. Try them fresh in a salad or sautéed, boiled, or fried. You can even visit a larger-than-life sculpture of a fiddlehead by sculptor Jim Boyd in St. John, New Brunswick.

PERSIANS

REGION: Ontario

A frosted sweet roll similar to a cinnamon bun, this pastry is available only in Thunder Bay, Ontario. The treats are topped with a distinctive pink frosting (the coloring is from strawberry or raspberry jam) and are apparently quite addictive: expats will pay enormous sums to have the pastries shipped to them. Invented in the 1940s by Art Bennett, founder of Bennett's Bakery, the treats were supposedly named after American general John "Black Jack" Pershing, who paid the bakery a visit. According to the Nucci brothers, who now own the place (and the nearby Persian Man coffee shop), they sell more than a hundred dozen persians a day.

GETTING SCREECHED IN

If you plan to spend any time in Newfoundland and Labrador, you'll want to be officially screeched in. This rite of passage involves kissing a dead cod fish—yep—and doing a shot of local rum. But not before the master of ceremonies asks you, "Are ye a screecher?"

The proper response? "'Deed I is, me ol' cock! And long may yer big jib draw!"

Add it to your bucket list.

Kiss the cod

HAIDA CANDY

REGION: British Columbia

Made from strips of cured, glazed, and smoked salmon, Haida candy, or salmon candy, is a traditional treat prepared by Indigenous nations on Canada's West Coast. The salmon is glazed with maple syrup, giving it a sweet, candied flavor. The sustainable Haida Wild Seafoods brand exports their own version of the treat across Canada.

STORM CHIPS

REGION: Maritimes

Originally the tongue-in-cheek name given by a CBC broadcaster to the snacks residents would stock up on before a big snowstorm (i.e., "Got to hit the grocery store for some #stormchips before the blizzard hits"), they're now an official kind of chip produced by Covered Bridge Potato Chips. What do they taste like? The brand promises a "flurry of flavours."

TIMBITS

REGION: Canada

A Timbit is a donut hole from the Canadian chain Tim Hortons. Whether you're a fan of this teeny-weeny donut or not—many Canadians lament the decline in the chain's donut quality over the years—the word *Timbit* is something you'll want to add to your vocabulary.

ALL-DRESSED, KETCHUP, AND DILL PICKLE POTATO CHIPS

REGION: Canada

Every Canadian brand of potato chips makes an all-dressed, ketchup, and a dill pickle version. All dressed is—you guessed it—all the flavors, while dill pickle and ketchup are just what they sound like. We're still not as advanced as England, with their prawn- or Sunday roast–flavored crisps, but we'll get there someday.

all dressed

COFFEE CRISP

REGION: Canada

This is a chocolate bar[12] made with crispy vanilla wafers and coffee-flavored candy covered in milk chocolate. Originally made in the United Kingdom and marketed as Wafer Crisp, this delicious snack is now made in Canada by Nestlé. Canadian expats were once so desperate to get their hands on their beloved Coffee Crisp that they petitioned the company to start exporting them—the bars were then briefly sold in the United States before reverting back to a Canadian-only confection.

KRAFT DINNER

REGION: Canada

"I'll never be able to give my kids a billion-dollar company, but Laureen and I are saving for their education. And I have actually cooked them Kraft Dinner—I like to add wieners."

—Former prime minister Stephen Harper

You're familiar with boxed macaroni and cheese. The kind that comes with the fluorescent orange cheese powder? You may even be

---

12 Canadians call them chocolate bars, not candy bars.

vaguely aware that Kraft is the name of the manufacturer. I'm here to tell you that in a bizarre coup for the Kraft marketing department, all Canadians refer to this as Kraft Dinner (its official name in Canada), and we eat it all the time. We consume 55 percent more Kraft Dinner than Americans. We write songs about it. Our prime ministers talk about it. Our pundits ponder its popularity. "What do you want for dinner, Samira?" "I want Kraft Dinner, Mom!" Welcome to Canada.

MILK IN A BAG

REGION: Mostly Ontario, Quebec, the Maritimes

So milk isn't uniquely Canadian, obviously. But the fact that many Canadians buy their milk in a plastic sack is a bit unusual. The bags of milk—they come in sacks of three—then fit inside a reusable plastic jug. Cut the tip of the milk bag with scissors (or a specialized milk-bag slicer), and pour your milk. Apparently, this quirk is the result of Canada switching to the metric system in the 1960s, when manufacturers determined it was easier to just inject milk into a bag than it was to rejig their machines to make liter cardboard milk cartons. It also happens to be much better for the environment.

The Sourtoe

THE STRANGE HISTORY OF CANADA'S WEIRDEST COCKTAIL

Canada's most well-known contribution to cocktail culture is, of course, the Caesar, but its *weirdest* is probably the Sourtoe Cocktail—which is saying something, considering the Caesar is made with juice from clams. The Sourtoe, from the Downtown Hotel in Dawson City, Yukon, is the stuff of myth and legend. And rightly so. Where else can you do a shot with an amputated toe in it?

This strange tradition supposedly started in 1973 after someone donated a preserved, frostbitten toe to the bar. Naturally, someone decided the toe belonged in a cocktail, and the Sourtoe was born. Anyone who's brave enough can sidle up to the bar and ask for the Sourtoe Cocktail. Simply choose your liquor of preference—Yukon Jack is

(continued on next page)

recommended—and the bartender will pour the shot and plop the desiccated toe into the glass. The only rule is as follows, according to local lore: "You can drink it fast, you can drink it slow, but your lips must touch the toe." So far, more than seventy thousand people have taken the toe challenge. Beware, though: there's a $2,500 fine for anyone who swallows it.

Over the years the toes have disappeared, fallen apart, or been swapped out for better-quality toes—so the bar does take donations. Donated toes (preferably the big one) are cured and preserved in accordance with health and safety regulations. In 2013 someone deliberately swallowed the toe. In 2017 someone just up and stole it; it was later mailed back to the bar with a note of apology. According to the bartender and toe master, Terry Lee, the toe "is an institution in Dawson. When someone frigs around with it, there goes our institution."

Sourtoe Cocktail

- 1 ounce 80-proof liquor of your choice

- 1 mummified human toe

- Courage

LAWS AND CUSTOMS:
Guns, Booze, and Blunts

The Canadian justice system is similar to those of other Western nations. We have local, provincial, and federal police (also known as the Royal Canadian Mounted Police, RCMP, or "Mounties") who enforce the laws and a generally well-functioning court system. A good rule of thumb is if it isn't legal in the United States, it likely isn't legal in Canada either (so if you came to Canada with plans to murder with impunity, you're out of luck). There are, of course, a few notable exceptions. Here we'll investigate the differences you'll need to know about.

SAME SEX MARRIAGE HAS BEEN LEGAL SINCE 2005

The Civil Marriage Act legalized same-sex marriage across Canada in 2005—though it was already legal in eight out of ten provinces and one of three territories. Canada was only the fourth country in the world to recognize same-sex unions. The United States followed ten years later, recognizing them in 2015.

GUN OWNERSHIP ISN'T A RIGHT

Anyone moving to Canada will need to leave their automatic weapons behind. Gun ownership in Canada is heavily regulated on the federal level, which means automatic weapons, handguns with a barrel of 10.5 centimeters or less, and modified shotguns, rifles, and handguns are all illegal. Most semi-automatic weapons are also banned. There's also nowhere in Canada that allows open carry. In other words, there is no right to bear arms in the great white north.

"It's true that the judgement of what firearms should be prohibited will be decided by the government of the day—and shouldn't it be that way?"

—Allan Rock, former justice minister

There's a logical reason for this. Unlike the United States, Canada never rose up to violently defeat its colonial overlords. We just held peaceful talks with Britain and eventually both parties agreed it was best that we become our own country. So the need for handguns just in case we need them for a civil uprising isn't something Canadians think about all that much. On the plus side, these regulations mean that Canada has less gun crime than the United States. According to data from Statistics Canada and the US Center for Disease Control, the United States saw more than 56,000 gun homicides between 2009 and 2013, while Canada saw 977 in the same period. That isn't to say we don't have horrific shootings here—we just have less of them. In 1989 a man murdered 14 women at a Montreal university in what's known as the École Polytechnique massacre. To date, it is the deadliest mass shooting in Canadian history.

Canadians do own guns: around 22 percent of Canadian households have one firearm, although just 2 percent of those households have a handgun—Canadians tend to own long guns for hunting and recreation purposes rather than for personal protection. Those who do legally possess guns are required to take safety courses and learn how to store and transport them correctly. So aside from ditching your weapons before you enter the country, be prepared for a different kind of gun culture: one that revolves around safety and regulation. And if you do possess a large collection of firearms that you don't want to part with—whether for personal protection, collectible, or doomsday purposes—then Canada may not be the place for you.

"We'll explain the appeal of curling to you if you explain the appeal of the National Rifle Association to us."

—Andy Barrie

MARIJUANA IS LEGAL

Smoke 'em if you got 'em

As of 2018 recreational marijuana is legal across Canada. That means adults can legally possess up to thirty grams (one ounce) of marijuana and share up to thirty grams with other adults. It's only the second country in the world to legalize cannabis, behind Uruguay. Each province is taking a different approach to sales and regulation, however, so it's your responsibility to learn what your options are and to ensure you're following the laws specific to your province. In most provinces you must be nineteen years old to buy or smoke it, except for Alberta and Quebec, where the legal age is eighteen. Generally, if you can't smoke tobacco somewhere, you won't be able to smoke cannabis there, either (just because pot is legal doesn't mean you can light up in an elementary school or hotbox your taxi). The police are also figuring out how to deal with people who illegally drive while high. Some provinces have privately run stores while others are run by the government. Some will allow you to grow your own plants, and others, like Quebec, won't.

Another important thing to keep in mind is that the US federal government considers marijuana to be a controlled substance: US border agents can deny entry to non-US citizens suspected of using or abusing marijuana and can also choose to deny entry to or detain anyone who works or invests in the industry. If you're traveling to the United States, leave your bud at home.

WE DO ALCOHOL A LITTLE BIT DIFFERENTLY

Canada briefly dabbled in prohibition in the 1920s, but alcohol is now gloriously legal in every province and territory—although it's generally not available *everywhere* like it is in the United States. The industry is still heavily regulated, so depending on where you live, you may not find beer at the corner store or in the grocery store. In Ontario, for example, booze is mainly available from the LCBO— (Liquor Control Board of Ontario) or from the Beer Store, as well as some grocery stores. This may sound like communist, nanny-state stuff, but the stores are very pretty and well stocked, and the booze profits help the government run the province, so everyone benefits from your aunt's gin habit.

Canadians produce great alcohol as well. We're mostly known for rye whisky and beer, but there's also a robust wine industry and lots of craft distilleries to suit every taste. The laws governing the legal age limit, whether you can drink in public, what stores can sell alcohol, and whether you're allowed to bring your own beer or wine to a restaurant all vary by province. In Alberta, Manitoba, and Quebec, for example, the legal drinking age is eighteen. Everywhere else you must be nineteen to drink legally. Liquor laws in Nunavut are the most stringent in Canada, with many dry areas and just one liquor store in the capital city of

rye whisky

Iqaluit. Driving with a blood alcohol limit of more than 0.80 is illegal across Canada, and penalties include losing your license and jail time. Don't drink and drive.

WE HAVE LANGUAGE LAWS

Every federal sign everywhere across Canada must be in both French and English. Except in Quebec, where the signs are in French only. Quebec laws are quite strict about this, which makes sense if you've learned your Quebec history. Requiring French on everything—even, famously, on menus at Italian restaurants—is a way of ensuring the French culture remains strong.

French stop sign → ARRÊT

FIVE MUST-WATCH CANADIAN HOCKEY MOVIES

"Canada is hockey."—NHL player Mike Weir

GOON. Watch it for all the sex and punching.

LES BOYS. Watch it because it's a classic French comedy and one of the most successful film series to come out of Quebec.

YOUNGBLOOD. Watch it because it stars Rob Lowe, Patrick Swayze, and Keanu Reeves in a story about junior hockey.

INDIAN HORSE. Watch it to learn the heartbreaking story of an Indigenous kid who grows up to play for the Toronto Maple Leafs.

Keanu on skates

THE SWEATER. Watch it because it's a delightful animated short based on one of Canada's most beloved children's books, *The Hockey Sweater* by Roch Carrier.

Match the History to the Famous Canadian Monument

1 This beautiful Catholic monument was built in Montreal in 1656. It's known for a series of stained-glass panels depicting the history of the city.

2 Located in Toronto, this radio tower is 1,815 feet tall and is the tallest building in the Western Hemisphere.

3 Canada's largest overseas war memorial, this soaring stone monument built in 1936 honors the soldiers who fought and died during World War I. The memorial is built on land that France granted to Canada in perpetuity.

4 Built in 1975 to honor Ukrainian settlers to the region, it's the largest of its kind in the world. The monument features 524 star patterns, 3,512 facets, 2,206 equilateral triangles, and 6,978 nuts and bolts.

5 This national historic site is home to one of the world's most beautiful and extensive private flower gardens. Along with the sunken garden, set in an old limestone quarry, there's a rose garden, Japanese garden, and Italian garden.

6 Although not a manmade monument exactly, this is perhaps the most famous landmark in Canada—with a drop of about 188 feet, daredevils have walked across it on a tightrope and gone over it in a barrel, with mixed results.

7 The largest 5-cent piece in all the land. Located in Sudbury, Ontario.

A. The Butchart Gardens

B. CN Tower

C. Canadian National Vimy Memorial

D. Big Nickel

E. Vegreville Egg

F. Horseshoe Falls

G. Notre Dame Cathedral

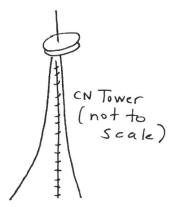

CN Tower (not to scale)

LANGUAGE: Terms to Know, and a Lesson in "Eh?"

Canadians speak hundreds of languages in their homes and communities, although for practical purposes, English is likely all you'll need to know unless you're traveling in rural Quebec or some Indigenous communities. Business is conducted in English as well, unless you're in Quebec or in the federal government, where everyone is expected to be fluent in both French and English. But just as Americans have their own regionalisms—I'm looking at y'all, South Carolina—so do Canadians.

THE EXTRA *U* AND THE *RE*—AND THE *C*

Canadian English is similar to British English, which means some words have an extra letter "u" and sometimes the "er" at the end of the word becomes "re." Sometimes a "c" becomes an "s" or a "q," and basically if you're unsure, just forget it, as even *we're* unsure of what's what anymore. And next time you want to honour your neighbour with some brightly coloured cupcakes, just ask yourself if the labour is worth it—last time that self-centred moustache-wearing mollusc complained about your fibre-rich, liquorice-flavoured treats. In your defence, you didn't realise they preferred savoury yoghurt to marvellous cupcakes.

CANADIAN WORDS, SLANG, AND OTHER REGIONALISMS

Buddy: friend or foe, depending on the inflection. If someone calls you buddy, they're either your friend for life or are about to beat you up. If you bump into someone and spill their beer, for example, and they shout, "Hey buddy, take 'er easy!" you better offer to buy them a new beer quickly. If you do, soon they'll be slinging an arm around your shoulders and letting people know, "My buddy here's okay."

Bunny hug: hoodie or sweatshirt in the prairie provinces

Bush party: party in a field somewhere, often with a bonfire, where someone from your high school is definitely getting alcohol poisoning

Bush party

"Keep Canada beautiful. Swallow your beer cans."

—Anonymous

Canadian Tire money: Monopoly money–looking coupons given out by national retailer Canadian Tire. People collect these things (with values of as little as 25 cents) and save up dozens or more to spend them. Or they keep them in a drawer until they die.

Canadian tuxedo: all-denim outfit

CBC: Canadian Broadcasting Corporation. It's a government-funded public broadcaster, like NPR, but watched and listened to by a vast spectrum of Canadians and not just wealthy liberals (sorry NPR) . Back in the day many rural areas could only get CBC radio stations, so generations of Canadians were raised on CBC programs.

Chesterfield: sofa or couch

Chinook: warm winter wind that blows through the Canadian Rocky Mountains

Chocolate bar: candy bar

College: a two-year trade school awarding diplomas and certificates. Although in the United States people use this term to refer to university, in Canada it means something specific. Keep this in mind when updating your résumé.

Deke: originally a hockey term, it means faking out or outmaneuvering your opponent

Double double: coffee from the Tim Hortons coffee chain, with two creams and two sugars

Elastic: a rubber band or hair tie. "Do you have an elastic? My toque messed up my hair" (see below).

Freezies: freeze pops or freezer pops

Fuddle duddle: f*ck you. This phrase was made famous by Prime Minister Pierre Trudeau in 1971, when members of Parliament claimed Trudeau had mouthed the words "f*ck off" to them in the House of Commons. Trudeau unconvincingly explained he may have said—or mouthed—"fuddle duddle or something like that."

Garburator: the garbage disposal unit in your kitchen sink

Group of Seven: Canada's most famous group of artists, collectively referred to as the Group of Seven. They were the first to paint Canada's landscapes in the 50s and 60s.

Lawren Harris

Highway: freeway

Humidex: measurement used to determine the effects of the combination of the heat and humidity. "The temperature is 28 degrees Celsius today, but with the humidex it will feel more like 35."

Hydro bill: electric or utility bill

Inuksuk or Inukshuk: a statue composed of loose stones that resembles a little person and traditionally used by the Inuit as a directional marker. These have become a Canadian symbol of sorts, and you can spot them on beaches and in front yards as decoration.

Keener: suck-up or brown-noser

Kitchen party: a traditional Newfoundland gathering with booze, friends, dancing, and live music. Usually held in someone's kitchen.

Klicks: kilometers

Knapsack: backpack

Loonie: one-dollar coin. It's called a loonie because one side depicts an image of a common Canadian bird, the loon.

Mickey: twelve-ounce bottle of liquor. "He drank a mickey before leaving the house, which is maybe why he barfed at the bush party."

Mountie: member of the Royal Canadian Mounted Police, so
named because they often appear on horses for ceremonial
events. This is Canada's federal police force.

Narwhal: unicorn of the sea. No, seriously,
this is a real arctic sea animal—a porpoise,
actually—with a tusk that can grow more
than eight feet long. Fun fact: the tusk
is technically a tooth and has millions of
nerve endings inside.

narwhal
(yes, really)

Pencil crayons: colored pencils

Pizza Pizza: the national pizza chain.
We do also have Pizza Hut and
Little Caesars, but Pizza Pizza rules
the land.

garlic
dipping
sauce

Pizza
Pizza

Pop: soda

Processed cheese: American cheese. Ask for American cheese in
Canada, and you'll be met with a blank stare. Whatever you call
it, it's like eating wet orange plastic.

Roll Up the Rim: a contest run seasonally by Tim Hortons wherein
you roll up the rim of your coffee cup to win—or, in my case,
never win—prizes like free coffee, cookies, or a car.

Runners: sneakers or tennis shoes. "Let's get off the chesterfield and get some exercise—go grab your runners!"

Serviette: napkin

Shawinigan handshake: a violent chokehold. This tongue-in-cheek term stems from an incident in which Shawinigan-born prime minister Jean Chrétien grabbed a protester by the neck, injuring him in the process. The photo and video of the incident went viral. A microbrewery even released a "Shawinigan Handshake" beer, with a label featuring Chrétien strangling hockey commentator Don Cherry.

Snowbird: Canadian retiree who moves south for the winter, usually to Florida

Snowbirds: either the plural of snowbird (see above) or a reference to the Canadian military aerobatic flight team. Currently consisting of eleven CT-114 Tutor airplanes, the Snowbirds perform at air shows and ceremonial events across Canada. Seeing them in action is really something.

Stag: bachelor party

Tap: faucet

Toboggan: sled

Toonie: two-dollar coin. "Do you have a toonie for the pop machine? Or two loonies? One pop costs two dollars."

Toque: knitted cap or beanie

University: a four-year school awarding undergraduate and graduate degrees

Two four: case of twenty-four beers

Washroom: bathroom or restroom

Wind chill: measurement used to determine the effects of both the cold and the wind. "The temperature is minus 8 degrees Celsius today, but with the wind chill it will feel more like a witch's tit."

Zed: the letter Z

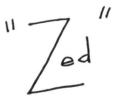

A LESSON IN *EH?*

Although it's one of the phrases most commonly associated with Canada, it's also the one outsiders misunderstand the most. So read on for how to correctly use the phrase "eh?"

"Eh?" comes at the end of a sentence, usually a statement, that you want people to agree with. In this case "eh?" is akin to "Don't you think?" Or it comes at the end of a statement that relays important information. So in this case "eh?" is more like "Did you know?" It's never used at the end of an actual question. F*cking this up is a classic way to demonstrate that you're not from Canada.

Eh?✓
EH! ✗

CORRECT

It's hot out today, eh?

Watch out for that
beaver, eh?

Man, buddy was really
givin' 'er,* eh?

I'm so obsessed with
hot dogs, eh?

INCORRECT

How's the weather today, eh?

Did the beaver wear a hat
on Saturday, eh?

Was buddy really
givin' 'er, eh?

I have some hot dogs, eh?
PROBABLY INCORRECT.
Even though this is a statement, it isn't a statement
you particularly need anyone to agree with. Unless
someone was lamenting the
fact that they had nothing
to eat and you're stating
that you have some spare
hot dogs and you'd like
them to know this fact.

*translation: givin' 'er =
trying hard at something*

NOTABLE CANADIANS
(Who Aren't Justin Trudeau or Justin Bieber)

A storied Canadian pastime is telling Americans which of their favorite celebrities are *actually* Canadian. So you probably already know that John Candy and Jim Carrey and William Shatner and Pamela Anderson and Samantha Bee are Canucks. And a Canadian will probably remind you again soon. But Canada is also full of notable people—politicians, activists, local artists— that you may not have heard about south of the border. Here are some of our national notables you might want to be familiar with.

Justin
(Trudeau + Bieber)

VIOLA DESMOND

Civil rights activist

The first person of color to appear on Canadian currency (as of 2018 her likeness graces the $10 bill, replacing the image of Canada's first prime minister), this civil rights pioneer has been compared to Rosa Parks. Desmond, a local businesswoman, made her stand in 1946 at

a Nova Scotia movie theatre, where she unknow-
ingly sat in a whites-only section. After refusing
to give up her seat, she was dragged out of the
theater, arrested, and jailed. She went to court to
appeal the conviction and lost—but the publicity
surrounding her case eventually led to the abo-
lition of segregation policies in the province. This was nine years
before Rosa Parks refused to sit at the back of the bus. Desmond
received a posthumous pardon in 2010.

NELLIE McCLUNG

Women's rights activist

This Canadian suffragette was instrumental in getting the government to formally acknowledge women as "persons" in 1927, which
then allowed women to run for office. She was famously quoted as
saying, "Never retract, never explain, never apologize; get things done
and let them howl." She was a total badass, and there's now a statue of
her on Parliament Hill in Ottawa.

SIR JOHN A. MACDONALD

Politician

"Let us be English or let us be French . . . but above all let us be Canadians."

—Sir John A. Macdonald

Canada's first prime minister was, at the time, a respected criminal lawyer who ushered in Confederation—uniting Upper and Lower Canada—and oversaw the construction of our national railway. He was also a drunk, a racist, and a corrupt politician (the sentiment quoted above didn't extend to the nation's Indigenous peoples, who he did his best to exterminate). Nevertheless, it's a fact that he was our first prime minister and that we're left to grapple with his legacy, which isn't that visible, to be honest. He served as prime minister for nineteen years, and yet, unlike his American counterpart George Washington, you'll find no cities named after him or major monuments in his honor. His face no longer appears on any currency. The few remaining statues in his likeness are currently the subject of debate as to whether they should be relocated to museums or allowed to stand where the pigeons can shit on them with impunity.

EMILY CARR

Artist

"It is wonderful to feel the grandness of Canada in the raw, not because she is Canada but because she's something sublime that you were born into, some great rugged power that you are a part of."

—Emily Carr

Emily Carr was one of Canada's first West Coast artists who, in the early 1900s, traveled alone—or with her pet dog or pet monkey—to many Indigenous communities up and down the coast of British Columbia, where she'd set up camp and paint. Often her paintings—featuring totem poles, villages, churches, and the surrounding forests—are the only visual record of those communities before disease or forced assimilation decimated them. She was also an accomplished author and won the Governor-General's Award in 1941 for her book *Klee Wyck*. She's now considered a Canadian icon and is one of Canada's best-known artists.

Emily Carr's

pet monkey

JACK LAYTON

Politician

Layton's
moustache

"My friends, love is better than anger. Hope is better than fear. Optimism is better than despair. So let us be loving, hopeful and optimistic. And we'll change the world."

—Jack Layton

Whatever side of the political aisle they were on, most Canadians liked and respected the late politician Jack Layton, federal leader of the left-leaning NDP. He was a hard-working, upbeat, lifelong public servant who got his start as a city councilor in Toronto, where he advocated for more affordable public housing and renewable energy initiatives. Known for his distinctive moustache, Layton was a cheerful, positive force in Canadian politics. His sudden death from cancer, shortly after his party achieved the best federal election outcome in its history, was a complete shock to the country and spurred a kind of public mourning the likes of which Canada had never seen before. The prime minister granted him a state funeral, which was attended by a wide range of politicians, including his friend and political adversary Rob Ford, also known as Toronto's crack-smoking mayor. The CN Tower and Niagara Falls were lit in NDP orange the day after his funeral.

PATRICK VINCENT (VINCE) COLEMAN

By no means a household name, Coleman nevertheless has a place in Canadian history for his role in helping to avert an incredible loss of life in the minutes leading up to the devastating Halifax explosion in 1917—an event that killed around two thousand people, injured nine thousand, and leveled much of the city. Despite knowing an explosion was imminent, the telegraph operator remained at his post, just a few hundred feet from the burning munitions ship, to send a warning message to an incoming passenger train. His message is purported to have said, "Hold up the train. Ammunition ship afire in harbor making for Pier 6 and will explode. Guess this will be my last message. Goodbye boys." This brought the passenger train and many other incoming trains that heard the warning to a halt. Coleman was killed in the explosion, but his actions saved hundreds of lives. His warning also allowed faraway railway operators to respond quickly by organizing trains full of doctors, nurses, and supplies to the devastated city. Most Canadians know his story from the Heritage Minute created in his honor.[13]

---

13 Look up Heritage Minutes, and watch all of them for a crash course in Canadian history. The videos are one-minute dramatizations of famous Canadian events and are produced by the government as a kind of feel-good propaganda. If you watched TV in Canada at any point in the nineties or early aughts, they're a pretty common reference point.

CHANIE WENJACK

Chanie's story is relatively new to most Canadians, but he's quickly become a symbol of the tragedy and violence the country's residential school system inflicted on Indigenous families. Chanie was a twelve-year-old Ojibwe boy who was forced to attend a Christian boarding school that was meant to assimilate Indigenous children into white culture. In October of 1966 Chanie escaped the school with a few of his friends and began the 600-kilometer (370-mile) journey back home. Wearing only a windbreaker and in freezing temperatures, he made it about 50 kilometers before succumbing to hunger and the elements. His death sparked an inquest that brought national attention to the plight of the children in the residential system and led to lawsuits and reforms. There is now a Heritage Minute in his honor as well.

TERRY FOX

Marathoner and cancer fund-raiser

This national icon is probably Canada's most famous athlete.[14] In 1980 cancer survivor Terry Fox began his cross-country Marathon of Hope to raise money for cancer research. With one leg amputated due to cancer, he ran with a prosthetic leg and a unique hopping gait. His east-west journey began in St. John's, Newfoundland, and he ran the equivalent

---

14 Props to Wayne Gretzky, too, I suppose.

of one marathon a day—*for more than four months.* Soon TV crews and thousands of cheering fans greeted Fox in each city he passed through. Unfortunately his cancer returned, and he was forced to abandon his journey just outside Thunder Bay, Ontario, to seek medical treatment. He'd run for an astonishing 143 days and 5,373 kilometers (3,339 miles). A national paper described the reaction to Fox's run as "one of the most powerful outpourings of emotion and generosity in Canada's history." When he died a year later the Canadian government ordered flags across the country to be lowered to half-mast. His legacy is massive—you'll find statues, schools, parks, and running trails named after him across Canada. The annual Terry Fox Run—with millions of participants in dozens of countries—is now the world's largest one-day fundraiser for cancer. As of 2018 more than $750 million for cancer research has been raised in his name. I dare you to find and watch a video of him running and not be moved to tears.

"It occurs very rarely in the life of a nation that the courageous spirit of one person unites all people in the celebration of his life and in the mourning of his death.... We do not think of him as one who was defeated by misfortune but as one who inspired us with the example of the triumph of the human spirit over adversity."

—Prime Minister Pierre Trudeau on Terry Fox

CHRIS HADFIELD

Astronaut

"Early success is a terrible teacher. You're essentially being rewarded for a lack of preparation, so when you find yourself in a situation where you must prepare, you can't do it. You don't know how."

—Chris Hadfield

You may already be familiar with Canada's favorite astronaut. Hadfield, a former Royal Canadian Air Force fighter pilot, shot to fame in 2013 for singing David Bowie's "Space Oddity" while on the International Space Station. The YouTube video has more than forty-one million views, and according to commenter EPIC-PIE-MAN, "This is what all of human history has led up to and it's the f*cking best thing in the universe." It really is. Hadfield also posted tons of mesmerizing videos demonstrating how astronauts washed their hands or brushed their teeth in space. He was also the first Canadian to walk in space.

LAURA SECORD

War heroine

Laura Secord was Canada's Paul Revere. Just as Revere rode through American villages to warn residents of the approaching British forces, so Secord raced to inform the British about a surprise American attack during the War of 1812. After learning of the Americans' plans, she walked twenty miles through American-occupied territory to warn British lieutenant James FitzGibbon and his forces. Her information helped the British and Mohawk warriors defeat the Americans at the Battle of Beaver Dams (a Canadian-sounding battle if there ever was one). Although her actions were little known during her lifetime, today Secord is a household name and the subject of plays, books, and poems—there is even a chocolate company named in her honor.

TOMMY DOUGLAS

Politician

"I don't mind being a symbol but I don't want to become a monument. There are monuments all over the parliament buildings and I've seen what the pigeons do to them."

— Tommy Douglas

Tommy Douglas was voted the country's number-one greatest Canadian in a CBC contest. The reason for this is that the premier of Saskatchewan was also the father of modern Medicare in Canada—and of course the universal health care system is something we're all very proud of.

DON CHERRY

Hockey commentator

A former NHL player and coach, Don Cherry has been a sports commentator for the CBC's *Hockey Night* in Canada for almost forty years. If you've watched a hockey game on TV in Canada, you've likely seen him, alongside his more reserved cohost Ron McLean, shouting his analysis into the camera. He's famous for his flamboyant, zany sense of style—watch for annual roundups of his most memorable blazers, which include very bright floral prints, skulls, blood spatters, and maple leaves. Cherry is also known for his love of a physical, rough kind of hockey (he released a massively popular series of videos called *Don Cherry's Rock 'Em Sock 'Em Hockey*) as well as his sometimes controversial comments (he once called Toronto cyclists "left-wing pinkos," for example). Cherry personifies a kind of unapologetic populism that's rarely seen in Canada (until recently) and that many find refreshing. He's a vocal supporter of the military and our veterans. He was also voted one of the country's greatest Canadians in a 2004 CBC poll, finishing seventh, ahead of Wayne Gretzky and the first prime minister, Sir John A. Macdonald, who came in tenth and eighth, respectively.

DAVID SUZUKI

"When we forget that we are embedded in the natural world, we also forget that what we do to our surroundings we are doing to ourselves."

—David Suzuki

Suzuki is an award-winning environmentalist of the highest order. The author of more than fifty books, he's also a professor and broadcaster, best known for his CBC television show *The Nature of Things*. He's also a documentarian and regularly speaks out about the dangers posed by climate change. Many Canadians grew up reading his children's books and learning how to reuse and recycle things like egg cartons into fun crafts our parents would pretend to find noteworthy.

VACATIONING LIKE
A CANADIAN

"A Canadian is someone who knows how to make love in a canoe."

—Pierre Trudeau

If you want to live here, you're going to have to learn how to vacation like a Canadian. Just like everyone else in the world, Canadians love to travel, learn new languages, and explore new cultures. Popular destinations for vacations include Europe, the Caribbean, and the United States. But unlike many other citizens around the globe, Canadians have a unique vacation style that's dictated by our cold winters. We love escaping our cold climate for southern sun. All-inclusive Mexican resorts basically run on Canadian dollars, and it's often cheaper to fly to Mexico than it is to somewhere within Canada. Find a patch of sunlight anywhere on Earth, and there will be a Canadian sunning themselves in it like a cat.

So read on to find out how to adapt your vacation style to the Canadian climate.

COTTAGING

Some Canadians are lucky enough to have had grandparents who were born in Canada. Those savvy grandparents often bought a piece of land up in "cottage country" (which in Ontario is basically any area within a day's driving distance of Toronto), where they built a primitive cottage—also called a camp, cabin, or lake house—on a lake. They likely left that cottage to their kids, who now also have kids who have kids. Today these cabins are highly sought after and have been renovated and rebuilt to become more like second homes—unaffordable to nearly everyone except those lucky enough to inherit one. Hopefully, though, you've got a friend with a cottage who will extend an invite to you so you can enjoy this quintessential Canadian experience.

Anyway, good luck to everyone today who inherited one-twenty-fourth of a cottage and has to coordinate the arrival dates of seven different families descended from the original grandparents every summer. No, *you're* bitter.

Quiz: What's Your Canadian Vacation Style?

1 When it comes to road trips, your opinion is:

    A. How else am I going to hit up every small-town museum, lighthouse, and roadside pie stand unless I'm driving?

    B. Top down, tunes up—let's hit up a beach in twelve hours!

    C. Windows up, air-conditioning on—until we get to the airport, where we will park and fly.

    D. It's difficult to get to my all-inclusive island vacation via car, so . . . no.

2 When it comes to souvenirs, you prefer:

    A. Locally published handbooks about ghost stories, old railways, and ship buildings

    B. Kitschy magnets, T-shirts, and conch shells with eyes glued on them

    C. Instagram photos of Joshua Tree National Park

    D. A sunburn and some duty-free rum or tequila

3 On vacation you like to meet and hang out with:

    A. Friendly locals

    B. Drunk spring breakers

    C. Hippies and retirees

    D. Other families with kids and honeymooners

4 Your perfect vacation meal consists of:

    A. Local lobster, clam chowder, and cider doughnuts

    B. Chicken fingers, burgers, and beer

    C. A date smoothie followed by some al pastor tacos

    D. An all-you-can-eat buffet and a frozen piña colada

5 When it comes to your preferred style of hotel, it's got to be:

    A. Roadside motel where you might get murdered. This is real Americana right here.

    B. Beachside. With a pool.

    C. A geodome in the desert powered by solar energy. I want to see the stars.

    D. A faux Mayan pyramid. Preferably with monkeys or peacocks running around.

(results on next page)

Mostly As: New England road trip: Bucking the trend of heading south, you prefer the scenery and culture of small-town America. You're a true original!

Mostly Bs: Florida and Myrtle Beach, South Carolina: You love the relaxed, anything-goes attitude of these vacation hot spots. Enjoy the beach with a drink in hand during the day and your favorite American chain restaurants at night. Plus, it's just a (relatively) short drive from the Canadian border!

Mostly Cs: Palm Springs, California, and Phoenix, Arizona: There's nothing like the unique landscape of US desert, and you're one of the thousands of Canadians who've discovered the new-age appeal of the hiking, hot springs, and drum circles in nearby Joshua Tree (if you're in Palm Springs) or the cool bars and arts district in downtown Phoenix. Of course, if bland condo timeshares and golf is more your thing, these spots have those in spades.

Mostly Ds: Mexico and the Caribbean: You only get a limited amount of vacation days, and you plan to spend them relaxing and getting a sunburn. You're here for the hot sun, the massive pool (and swim-up bar), and the knowledge that everything is all inclusive.

Quiz: Test Your Knowledge of Canada

How well do you know the Great White North? Remember, Canadians are known for their upstanding character—so no cheating!

1 What was the name of Canada's first prime minister?

    A. Sir John A. McDonald

    B. Lester B. Pearson

    C. Joe Clark

    D. Kim Campbell

2 What is Canada's national animal?

    A. Loon

    B. Canada goose

    C. Beaver

    D. Moose

3 How many countries border Canada?

    A. One: The U.S.

    B. Three: The U.S., Russia, and Greenland

    C. Zero

    D. None of the above

(continued on next page)

4 Which province was the last to join Canada in 1949?

A. Nunavut

B. Newfoundland and Labrador

C. Calgary

D. Prince Edward Island

5 What is the capital city of Canada?

A. Montreal

B. Ottawa

C. Toronto

D. Vancouver

6 What is the name of Canada's only major league baseball team?

A. Montreal Expos

B. Toronto Blue Jays

C. Edmonton Egrets

D. Hamilton Tiger Cats

7 What country or countries are larger than Canada by land mass?

A. United States

B. United States and Russia

C. Russia and China

D. Russia

8 Why is Laura Secord famous?

A. She was a civil rights pioneer and now appears on the ten-dollar bill

B. She warned British soldiers the Americans were coming during the War of 1812

C. She was the first woman to swim across Lake Ontario

D. She founded a famous chocolate company

9 A leaf from which tree is featured on Canada's flag?

A. Oak

B. Maple

C. Birch

D. Tamarack Larch

10 What is the name of Canada's national anthem?

A. "God Save the Queen"

B. "My Heart Will Go On"

C. "O Canada"

D. "Maple Leaf Forever"

(continued on next page)

11 Who appears on all of Canada's currency?

    A. Bob and Doug McKenzie

    B. The Queen

    C. Justin Trudeau

    D. Bucky Beaver

12 What is/are Canada's official language or languages?

    A. English

    B. English and French

    C. English and Inuktitut

    D. Chesterfield

13 What city is nicknamed "Hollywood North" due to its robust film industry?

    A. Toronto

    B. Vancouver

    C. Niagara Falls

    D. Halifax

14 Canada Day falls on what day of the year?

    A. June 1st

    B. July 4th

    C. January 14th

    D. July 1st

⑮ Canada uses the metric system. Which of the following statements is correct?

    A. It was 32 degrees Celsius when I walked 2 kilometres for a 32-ounce soda pop.

    B. I drank about a litre of vodka and must have fallen 3 metres down that hole.

    C. I drove 23 miles to buy ten grams of legal marijuana.

    D. An adult elephant weighs about 5 tons and the average baby weighs about 8 pounds at birth.

RESULTS:

0-5 points: Read this book again.

6-10 points: Think you're pretty smart, eh?

10-13 points: Let me tell you about the secret Canadian handshake. You've earned it.

Acknowledgments

Many thanks to Jessica Riordan, my amazing editor at Running Press, for coming to me with this idea, and to Julie Matysik for recommending me for the project. Thanks to Susan Van Horn, Josephine Moore, Hope Clarke, and Kendra Millis, as well as the marketing, publicity, sales, and distribution team at Running Press. Much love to the independent bookstores who make books like this possible. Many thanks to the Canadians in my online writing group for all the regional recommendations about which artists to read, watch, and listen to in each province. Thanks to the staff at the Brooklyn UPS store, who didn't laugh while scanning my moose and Fidel Castro doodles. Thanks to all the beautiful people who welcomed my parents to Canada many years ago and to everyone in Canada working to make the world a welcoming, accepting, and friendly place.

Index

175

About the Author

GREG NAESETH

JENNIFER McCARTNEY is the *New York Times* bestselling author of *The Joy of Leaving Your Sh*t All Over the Place* and several other books. Born and raised in Hamilton, Ontario, she currently lives in Brooklyn, New York. She is a dual Canadian and American citizen.